That's Not What The Bible Says

Unraveling Common Misconceptions For Better Biblical Understanding

E.O. Valle

That's Not What The Bible Says

Copyright © 2023 by E.O. Valle

ISBN: 979-8-9891602-4-2 (Paperback)
ISBN: 979-8-9891602-5-9 (Hardcover)
ISBN: 979-8-9891602-3-5 (eBook)

Scripture quotations are from The ESV® Bible (The Holy Bible, English Standard Version®), © 2001 by Crossway, a publishing ministry of Good News Publishers. Used by permission. All rights reserved.

Scripture quotations marked (NIV) are taken from the Holy Bible, New International Version®, NIV®. Copyright © 1973, 1978, 1984, 2011 by Biblica, Inc.™ Used by permission of Zondervan. All rights reserved worldwide. www.zondervan.com, The "NIV" and "New International Version" are trademarks registered in the United States Patent and Trademark Office by Biblica, Inc.™

Scripture taken from the New King James Version®. Copyright © 1982 by Thomas Nelson. Used by permission. All rights reserved.

Scriptures marked with KJV are taken from the King James Version, public domain.

All rights reserved.

No portion of this book may be reproduced in any form without written permission from the publisher or author, except as permitted by U.S. copyright law.

Introduction

I remember the first time it happened to me – one sentence, thirteen words, said by someone who didn't look it but must have been crazy. It was the most ridiculous thing I had ever heard as a Christian. I almost dismissed him, but somehow, I couldn't. I can still recall his exact words, "The Bible does not teach that when we die, we go to heaven."

What?! Of course, we go to heaven. Everyone knows that. Where on earth did he get that notion from?

The possibility drove me a bit nuts, and I had to find out for myself. Surprisingly, it didn't take very long. To my chagrin, the man wasn't crazy after all. He had simply done his homework. And then I thought, "What else do I believe that isn't true?"

I think we can all agree that having bad directions will get us to places we don't want to be.

What if having incorrect information is affecting our faith walk? Are we fighting life battles that we shouldn't be fighting? What if our salvation or kingdom rewards are at risk because of what we are doing or not doing due to faulty understanding?

Eternity is too important to have the attitude that says, "I think this is the way." We ought to be sure. And that is just as true for this life on earth.

My biblical journey began with those questions. They awoke an appetite in me that I never imagined I could have for anything, much less the Bible. I wanted and needed to know what it said and taught, so my research began. That process included going back to school for a divinity degree. It was one of my best decisions as it broadened my views on the historical and philosophical influence of Christianity, which I would later need in my investigation. In almost a decade, I've spent countless hours reading and studying scripture, cross-referencing thoughts and ideas, listening to sermons, pouring through commentary, and fact-checking everything and anything that sounded even a little bit different from what I thought to be true.

I was amazed at how many things I found and still continue to find – ideas and values of the Christian faith that are not taught in the Bible. In this book, I share some of those findings. Not just with summarized conclusions but with verse-by-verse evidence.

The purpose of this book is to show the importance of making the Bible your ultimate source for understanding God, His character, and His plan for humanity – and for you specifically. This is done by showing numerous examples of things that we have been taught or have learned about these topics that are not Biblical.

Much of what many of us know or believe about God, Christianity, and anything related to the Bible, comes from sermons, devotionals, movies, and secondhand information. We all benefit from the time that others have dedicated to studying and who have shared their findings with us. I pray that we never lack those people in this world. However, if there is anything that I've learned in all my years of study, it is to always check the facts. The intention is not to take on or challenge any scholar, pastor, Bible teacher, or institution. I simply aim to encourage you, the reader, to use the Bible as your ultimate source of truth.

My methodology varies depending on the topic, although several approaches are consistent throughout. Other than employing the basic rules of interpretation as I understand them, there are two things that I heavily rely on. The first is the entirety of the Bible, not just selected verses. This entails finding and examining every iteration of a particular word or phrase in the Bible to determine commonalities and exceptions. Whether there are 50 or 250, every verse is considered. This includes using various Bible versions since a word could be translated differently from one version to the next.

The second is what I call the "fight the urge" rule. That is, fighting the urge to read too quickly, ignoring "inconsequential" words, and coming to conclusions without solid evidence. Mostly, it's fighting the urge to lean on an old understanding that I've never proven with scripture myself.

Why should you read this book? Many readers will be surprised by what they will learn in these pages. But more than for this new knowledge, you should read this book to get a sense of how much you could be missing if the Bible is not your ultimate source of understanding. Things that could have eternal consequences.

If you can recall the story of Moses and vividly see him floating down the Nile as a baby in a basket, this book is for you – that never happened.

Contents

1. The Afterlife: A Biblical Perspective on Death   2
2. Contradictory Views on The Afterlife   28
3. The Deeper Meaning of Biblical Fasting   68
4. The Many Facets of Baptism   89
5. Unearthing the Purpose of Jesus' Baptism   121
6. The Golden Rule as Defined by Jesus   133
7. Exploring Fruit-Bearing Salvation   143
8. Reconsidering Divine Exclusivity on Being Good   159
9. Rethinking The Good Samaritan Parable   173
10. Samaria: Ancient Jewish Travel Myths   188

Methodology   203

About the Author   209

Acknowledgements

Many are the people who have contributed to this book. Most unknowingly, through countless questions, conversations, and debates regarding scripture and the nature of God — always pushing me to return to the Biblical text to find the truth (you know who you are). These interactions account for most of the topics in this book. The number of people is significant, and I fear that if I start listing the names, I will fail to list them all. If you have ever had one of these conversations with me, have prodded me with Biblical questions, or have been part of any of the group Bible studies that I have led, please know that I have you in mind, and I thank you from the bottom of my heart.

There are others who I would like to mention by name whose contributions came in a different form.

We all need at least one person in our lives who inspires us. Either through constant encouragement or by being an example. Ideally, it is someone who does both. For me, that person is Janet Braen. Her presence in my life has been a source of inspiration throughout my ministry journey. The faith she has shown in me and her endless encouragement and support has been a powerful force that has fueled my passion for ministry and the writing of this book. Her confidence in my abilities empowered me to grow as a teacher and deepen my own faith. Her impact on my life and work has been immeasurable.

The second person is someone who never lets me forget that whatever fears I may have of failing or falling are irrational – simply because she would never let them happen. With that matter-of-fact attitude, Lydia Spingler consistently reminds me that not only is God's hand on my life but that I have people around me that I can count on when things get tough. Her words always help me clear a path in my thinking to push forward to do what needs to get done.

The next two individuals are Paul Flynn and John Kim. These men have been part of my accountability team for quite some time, and I could not be more thankful for them. Paul is the guy who always tells me what I don't want to hear. It is both frustrating and satisfying at the same time. I never have to wonder that his words will come sugarcoated. I can count on his assessment as always being untainted. John's encouragement comes in the way of challenging me to consider things I may have missed and, like Paul, always pulls me in to uncover the whole truth. Together, they bring a level of encouragement that is pure gold. Not by applause but by reminding me that being lazy with the Word of God is never an option.

On the technology front, I've been blessed to work with Orazio Lentini and Carlos Albuquerque, the brilliant minds behind the software development team responsible for our websites, the companion Bible Study Library, and the Bible Dose online platform. Their exceptional work was instrumental in bringing all the online components together. Their unwavering commitment to their craft allowed me to focus on completing the book and not have to worry about the supporting technology.

I would like to express my heartfelt gratitude to the two independent editors, Barbara Bowen and Lynette Stewart, for their invaluable contribution. Their dedication, expertise, and keen eye for detail have greatly enriched my work. I thank them for helping me bring my vision to life.

For the Spanish translation of the book, I have Pastor Amadeo Albuquerque to thank. Pastor Amadeo holds a Master of Divinity and a Master of Religious Education, as well as a Bachelor of Education Sciences, with a specialization in Spanish. His encouragement and affirmation of the theological principles presented herein were a great source of inspiration and motivation during this journey.

For the audiobook, I was blessed to connect with Pastor Jonathan Broscious who besides being the Campus Pastor of New Hope Church also has nearly 20 years of radio, voice tracking, podcasting, voice-over, and public speaking experience. Not only did he bring a perfect voice to the project but because of his understanding of scripture was able to present the content in the form that it was intended.

I thank God for putting all of these individuals in my life and for giving me the privilege to serve Him daily. This book is yet another testament to His unending grace.

Dedication

To my beloved mother, Aura, who gave me unconditional love, taught me how to laugh, and paved the way for my walk with God.

PART 1
Where do we go When we Die?

CHAPTER ONE

The Afterlife: A Biblical Perspective on Death

The topic of our mortality and what happens when we die has been discussed and debated for more years than any of us probably realize, both within the realm of faith and outside of it. As Christians, we believe in an afterlife promised to us by God. It is what awaits us on the other side of God's saving grace. The Bible is clear on this point. The how, the when, and the where, however, stir up quite the debate.

Where does a person go when they die? Is it heaven? If it is, do they leave immediately after dying, or is there a waiting period? Is there consciousness?

First and foremost, asking this multi-part question in this manner presumes that some part of us can and does somehow live apart from the body after the body dies. Therefore, whatever this thing is, we must necessarily conclude that it is immortal. How else can it live beyond the physical body unless it is immortal? Of course, we are referring to the soul.

Also, let us observe the question itself. Purposefully, the question here is being asked in a popular fashion (or in similar words), "Where does a person go when they die?" Rarely does anyone ask where the soul goes. Instead, they ask where the person goes. Why is that? Could it be because, for most of us, our fuzzy understanding is that our soul is what makes us a person, and so when we say *person*, we really mean *soul*?

One of the more popular views on death is that when a person dies, the soul is swept away to a better place. Many Christians believe that this place is heaven. Oddly enough, even some non-Christians believe their destination is heaven. But is that what the Bible says?

The shortest verse in the Bible

The shortest verse in the English-translated Bible is found in John 11:35, where it reads, *"Jesus wept."* It is located in the story of Lazarus, a close friend of Jesus, who dies and is resurrected by Jesus four days after his death.

I once heard someone say that Jesus wept because He was sorrowful that He was bringing Lazarus back from heaven, where the streets are paved with gold, and returning him to this broken world. One could imagine Jesus torn between leaving Lazarus in a state of perfect bliss in heaven or returning him to his grieving family. As touching as that might sound, as we will see shortly, it is not likely the reason why Jesus wept.

Everyone wants to believe that when a loved one dies, they go straight to heaven. Or at least a place that is better than Earth. If you've ever attended a funeral ceremony, you undoubtedly heard someone say, "He or she is in a better place now." Even if the person had no relationship with God or was far from being what we might consider a "good" person, loved ones cannot imagine their deceased being anywhere other than somewhere like paradise.

Let us look at a few passages in scripture that will shed some light on where we go when we die, if anywhere at all, and when it is that we get there.

Awakening from the tombs

We will begin with a passage from Jesus speaking about Himself:

> *Do not marvel at this, for an hour is coming when all who are in the tombs will hear his voice and come out, those who have done good to the resurrection of life, and those who have done evil to the resurrection of judgment. (John 5:28-29 ESV)*

Notice the similarity between Jesus' words and those of Daniel in the Old Testament:

> *Multitudes who sleep in the dust of the earth will awake: some to everlasting life, others to shame and everlasting contempt. (Daniel 12:2 NIV)*

Both passages speak about the same end-times event and prompt us to ask two questions. If people go to heaven immediately after death, as some believe, who exactly is in the tombs that will hear Jesus' voice and come out, and who are asleep in the dust of the earth that will awake? The passages clearly refer to both Christians and non-Christians, so the obvious conclusion is that no one goes to heaven, or anywhere else for that matter when they die. Instead, all who die remain in the grave until Jesus' second coming.

Of course, given the questions that we are attempting to answer, there is an objection here; if indeed the soul is immortal then Jesus and Daniel might be referring to the dead bodies that are in the graves, not the souls. The assumption is that the soul is with God in heaven and that at the resurrection of the body, they will be reunited. But does that even make sense? If the soul is active in heaven, we assume it can "hear," and if dead bodies will also rise and "hear," then aren't we talking about two different beings? How can the soul and the body be alive separate from each other? Does one of them rule over the other?

As we continue, we will have to consider this point: the immortality of the soul, something that lives without the body.

The last day

In the Book of John, there is an account of Jesus, Who is in Capernaum, teaching about being the bread of life. During His discourse, Jesus is asked, *"What must we do to do the works God requires?"* This is Jesus' response:

> *For this is the will of my Father, that everyone who looks on the Son and believes in him should have eternal life, and I will raise him up on the last day. (John 6:40 ESV)*

Four times in John 6, speaking of believers, Jesus says, *"I will raise them up in the last day."* Again, we are faced with the same question. If Christians go to heaven immediately after death, who exactly is Jesus raising up on the last day? Claiming that the soul is immortal would allow a person to interpret Jesus' words to mean that He is raising up dead bodies, not souls.

Concerning the "last day" that Jesus mentions, it does not mean the last day of a person's life. The last day refers to the end of this world as we know it. When Lazarus died and Jesus was speaking to his sister Martha, we read this exchange:

> *Jesus said to her, "Your brother will rise again." Martha said to him, "I know that he will rise again in the resurrection on the last day." (John 11:23-24 ESV)*

It sounds like Martha is not thinking that Lazarus is somehow "alive" somewhere, in heaven, or anywhere else. Her understanding seems to be that Lazarus is dead in the grave and that he will be there until the last day when he will be finally resurrected.

Still, was Martha correct in thinking that Lazarus was dead in the grave, and not somewhere else in an awake or conscious state? Let's read how Jesus responds:

> *Jesus said to her, "I am the resurrection and the life. He who believes in Me, though he may die, he shall live. And whoever lives and believes in Me shall never die. Do you believe this?" (John 11:25-26 ESV)*

Hmm, well this is confusing. Jesus says that those who believe in him "though he may die, he shall live." This confirms that first the person dies, and then they live. But then he says that whoever believes never dies. The first part sounds like a resurrection, but what about "never dies?" Some might assume that Jesus is referring to the soul as the part that never dies, thereby having a case for the immortality of the soul. But would that be correct?

For this, we need to expand our view beyond the words themselves and consider the writing style and structure. Most of us, especially in the West, are not familiar with the different styles found in Biblical writings, so we fail to consider how they might affect the actual meaning of the words. This often leads us to strained interpretations.

Let us look at Jesus' first sentence. It has two parts: *I am the resurrection,* and *I am the life.* This is followed by two other sentences, each corresponding to the two parts in the first sentence. Broken apart and reassembled, it would look like this:

I am the resurrection . . . *He who believes in Me, though he may die, he shall live.*

I am the life . . . *And whoever lives and believes in Me shall never die.*

Do you see it? Because He is the resurrection, He will bring to life those who die, and because He is the life, anyone who is alive when He comes will not experience death. The message here is not that the soul is immortal; it's that Jesus has authority over life and death.

Paul's letter to the Thessalonians

In the first letter to the Thessalonians, we read these words of encouragement from Paul about relatives who have passed away, or as it is commonly referred to, "fallen asleep."

> *But we do not want you to be uninformed, brothers, about those who are asleep, that you may not grieve as others do who have no hope. For since we believe that Jesus died and rose again, even so, through Jesus, God will bring with him those who have fallen asleep. (1 Thessalonians 4:13-14 ESV)*

The second sentence says that God will bring with Him those who have fallen asleep. We might be tempted to think that the statement means that He is bringing them from heaven where their souls have been "living" or "awake" since the body's death. But that would be ignoring the first sentence where we can clearly see that he is referring to those who are asleep. In other words, those who died and are still dead.

Paul goes on to explain how God will bring them:

> *For the Lord himself will descend from heaven with a cry of command, with the voice of an archangel, and with the sound of the trumpet of God. And the dead in Christ will rise first. Then we who are alive, who are left, will be caught up together with them in the clouds to meet the Lord*

*in the air, and so we will always be with the Lord.
(1 Thessalonians 4:16-17 ESV)*

We notice that Paul says that they will rise (future tense) before the living meet up with them. And finishes with *"we will always be with the Lord."* Not that we are always with the Lord, but that we will be.

We also notice that there is no mention of souls. Paul speaks of Jesus coming, the dead rising, and the living being taken up. However, there is no mention of a soul, and certainly nothing about a coming together of soul and body. One would think that this would have been the perfect time for Paul to tell us about this "reunion of soul and body" if, indeed, there was such a thing. Could it be that when Paul said that the dead would rise, he never imagined such a thing as an immortal soul separate from a body?

There is more to be observed. The idea that we go directly to be with the Lord in some kind of conscious state when we die comes mostly from Paul's writings. Not that Paul said it, but that people interpret some of his writings that way. Yes, there are a few other passages that seem to suggest the idea, but it is from Paul's letters that most people extract their evidence. We will cover more of that further below. In the meantime, we must ask the obvious question: if Paul really believed that when we die, we go directly to be with the Lord in some conscious state, then why didn't he bring that up in this letter to the Thessalonians?

This letter is meant to encourage the Thessalonians. They are concerned about their loved ones who have passed away, wanting to know what would become of them. Why didn't Paul just say, "Hey guys, don't worry about your loved ones;

they are already with the Lord just waiting for you to join them?" Instead, he goes into this picturesque account of the return of Jesus, who will, at some later time, resurrect the dead and join them with the living.

The dead don't praise the LORD

The Psalmist of chapter 115 writes a beautiful poem. Its aim is to give God glory. It calls for Israel, the house of Aaron, and all those who fear the LORD to give Him praise . . . for the dead do not.

> *The dead do not praise the LORD, nor do any who go down into silence. (Psalm 115:17 ESV)*

If we assume that a person's soul goes to be with the Lord when their body dies, why would they not praise the LORD? According to this Psalmist, the answer is simple: because they are dead, and the dead have no consciousness. Is that not the point that the Psalmist is making?

David, too, uses the same reasoning in his poem as he cries out to God to deliver his life. "Be gracious to me," says David, "deliver my life . . . because dead, I have no memory of you; in the grave, I can't praise you." (Paraphrased.) These are his actual words:

> *Turn, O LORD, deliver my life; save me for the sake of your steadfast love. For in death there is no remembrance of you; in Sheol who will give you praise? (Psalm 6:4-5 ESV)*

Heman the Ezrahite, in his Psalm, takes it a step further as he makes his case before God while in great despair. He is so overwhelmed that he feels like he's dying. He pleads with God to save him from that death because, like David said in his Psalm, "I can't praise you if I'm dead."

> *You have put away my acquaintances far from me; You have made me an abomination to them; I am shut up, and I cannot get out; My eye wastes away because of affliction. LORD, I have called daily upon You; I have stretched out my hands to You. Will You work wonders for the dead? Shall the dead arise and praise You? Selah*
>
> *Shall Your lovingkindness be declared in the grave? Or Your faithfulness in the place of destruction? Shall Your wonders be known in the dark? And Your righteousness in the land of forgetfulness? (Psalm 88:8-12 NKJV)*

In the last two verses, Heman asks God four questions regarding the dead and their awareness of the Holy One. They are all rhetorical questions, and the answer to each is no. The dead are not aware of God's wonders. The dead do not rise up to praise. They do not feel God's love. Neither are His faithfulness or righteous deeds seen by them. It's difficult to read these words and not conclude that in death, there is no consciousness.

Of course, we have not yet resolved the idea that perhaps the psalmist is only speaking about dead bodies and not about souls (we are getting to that). But even before we get there, does it even make sense that the psalmist would be making such a big deal about dead bodies if souls were in fact somewhere praising God?

Traditionally, it is believed that Solomon, the son of David and the wisest man in the Bible, wrote the Book of Ecclesiastes. This is what he says about the dead:

> *For the living know that they will die, but the dead know nothing, and they have no more reward, for the memory of them is forgotten. Their love and their hate and their envy have already perished, and forever they have no more share in all that is done under the sun. (Ecclesiastes 9:5-6 ESV)*

> *Whatever your hand finds to do, do it with your might, for there is no work or thought or knowledge or wisdom in Sheol, to which you are going. (Ecclesiastes 9:10 ESV)*

These passages are affirmation that the dead are dead, without consciousness of any kind, and able to do nothing. There is no thought or knowledge or wisdom and no one is praising God. This does not refer to just the body being dead. We know this because it speaks of thinking, feeling, hating, and loving. These are not physical things, these are things that occur in the inner self, what we might call the soul.

Job is really dead

In the Book of Job, while Job is in agony over his circumstances and condition, he petitions God to consider ending his life. Just prior to that petition, he says this:

> *But a man dies and is laid low; man breathes his last, and where is he? As waters fail from a lake and a river wastes away and dries up, so a man lies down and rises not again; till the heavens are no more he will not awake or be roused out of his sleep. (Job 14:10-12 ESV)*

Job tells us that a dead man is dead. Once he breathes his last, all is lost, hence the words, "and where is he." He will not rise again till the heavens are no more. He will not awake until that time. Since that time has not yet come, we can safely say that Job is dead, not awake or roused from his sleep, as is with everyone else who has passed away.

This passage has been widely interpreted in very interesting ways, especially by some who believe that the soul continues to live beyond the death of the body. One such interpretation is that Job was only referring to never awakening back to the land of the living, the earth. Leaving us to assume that he would go on to a different realm somehow. But that does not seem to match Job's words here nor words from a previous passage when he was cursing the day he was born. Let us go there:

> *Why did I not die at birth, come out from the womb and expire? Why did the knees receive me? Or why the breasts, that I should nurse? For then I would have lain down and been quiet; I would have slept; then I would have been at rest,* (Job 3:11-13 ESV)

Again, we see the idea of being asleep and at rest. It seems clear that Job is not thinking that upon death he would be moving on to some existence or another body or other place. The future that he sees is not one of new beginnings or activity but one without thought or consciousness.

Another "colorful" way to express this idea is found in the writings of Jeremiah when he pens his sorrows in the Book of Lamentations.

> *he has made me dwell in darkness like the dead of long ago.* (Lamentations 3:6 ESV)

Jeremiah is not distinguishing the righteous from the wicked. He is referring to all those who have died before him. Those who are dead, even from long ago, dwell in darkness. Is there any darkness in heaven? Since the answer to that is no, then it stands to reason that Jeremiah is not picturing the dead in heaven or any other place other than the grave.

Daniel, Abraham, Moses, and Joshua are all dead

In Daniel's vision, God was telling him about things to come in end times. The last thing in that vision was God telling

Daniel about his future. These are the ending words in the Book of Daniel:

> *But go your way till the end. And you shall rest and shall stand in your allotted place at the end of the days. (Daniel 12:13 ESV)*

Notice that God doesn't tell Daniel that when he dies, he would be whisked to heaven. Instead, He tells him that he would rest until the end of days, and at that time, he would then stand in his allotted place. These words, from God Himself, echo the sentiment we just read in Job. This is similarly true of Abraham and his conversation with God when He tells Abraham how things end for him.

> *As for you, you shall go to your fathers in peace; you shall be buried in a good old age. (Genesis 15:15 ESV)*

One can try to argue that Abraham's fathers were in heaven and that's where God was saying that he was going, but that would be a huge assumption since there really isn't anything in scripture to support that. Additionally, since God resides in heaven, wouldn't it have been more appropriate for Him to say, "You will come to your fathers" instead of "You shall go to your fathers?"

Notice how similar the words are that God uses with Moses when He gives him the same message about his end.

> *And the LORD said to Moses, "Behold, you are about to lie down with your fathers…" (Deuteronomy 31:16 ESV)*

If consciousness existed after death, it would seem strange to tell Moses that he would *"lie down with his fathers."* Similar words were said to Joshua in the Book of Judges. In these places and others, Scripture tells us that these greats were all gathered to their ancestors (or fathers), but not once does it mention going to heaven.

In this Psalm, the author is making the point that the fate of the rich is the same as everyone else's — eventual death. And whatever they achieve is not going with them.

> *For though, while he lives, he counts himself blessed — and though you get praise when you do well for yourself — his soul will go to the generation of his fathers, who will never again see light. (Psalms 49:18-19 ESV)*

Notice that the psalmist says that it is the soul that goes to his fathers, not the body — and let us not miss the part about never again seeing light.

Jesus is coming, we are not going

What did Jesus tell His disciples? He said that He was going to prepare a place for them and that He would be back for them, not that they would come to Him.

> *In my Father's house are many rooms. If it were not so, would I have told you that I go to prepare a place for you? And if I go and prepare a place for you, I will come again and will take you to myself, that where I am you may be also. (John 14:2-3 ESV)*

Not that the other verses are not convincing enough, but let's consider this one thoroughly because some might say that Jesus is referring to coming back for their dead bodies. Inspecting the words carefully, we read that Jesus tells His disciples that He is returning to get them. He doesn't say, "I'm coming back to get your bodies." He says, "I'm coming back to get YOU!"

Peter agrees that salvation is not for dead bodies in the ground. While writing about the living hope of believers to eternal life he pens this:

> *obtaining the outcome of your faith, the salvation of your souls. (1 Peter 1:9 ESV)*

Notice the use of the word *soul*. Peter uses it exactly as we have been describing all along. This also supports Jesus' words.

For more support of the idea that bodies are not what are being resurrected, we have this Psalm that mentions explicitly that it is the whole of the person (soul) that will be ransomed, not just the body.

> *But God will ransom my soul from the power of Sheol, for he will receive me. Selah (Psalms 49:15 ESV)*

By now, we should be getting a clear picture that when a person dies, no part of them goes directly to heaven, including the "soul", and that there is no consciousness of any kind. And yet, there is more.

Immortality

We have looked at many scripture verses that support the idea that upon death there is no more consciousness of any kind. If you are still not convinced, it is probably because you believe that the soul is something separate from the body and that it is immortal. Believing that forces you to restrict all those passages that we have seen to mean that they are referring to the body only and not the soul. Let's see what the Bible says.

The word *immortal* appears in the Bible just seven times, and all seven times it is used exclusively by the apostle Paul. This is interesting because, as we mentioned previously and which we will cover again later, his writings are what people turn to for "proof" that when we die, we go directly to heaven, inferring that the soul is immortal. Let's see what Paul actually says.

In Paul's first letter to Timothy, Paul charges Timothy to fight the good fight of faith. In this account in chapter two, Paul mentions eternal life in one verse and immortality in another. Notice how Paul distinguishes one term from the other. And notice how he assigns the terms and to whom.

> *But as for you, O man of God, flee these things. Pursue righteousness, godliness, faith, love, steadfastness, gentleness. Fight the good fight of the faith. Take hold of the eternal life to which you were called and about which you made the good confession in the presence of many witnesses. I charge you in the presence of God, who gives life to all things, and of Christ Jesus, who in his testimony before Pontius Pilate made the good confession, to keep the commandment unstained and free from reproach until the appearing of our Lord Jesus Christ, which he will display at the proper time—he who is the blessed and only Sovereign, the King of kings and Lord of lords, who alone has immortality, who dwells in unapproachable light, whom no one has ever seen or can see. To him be honor and eternal dominion. Amen. (1 Timothy 6:11-16 ESV)*

Did you catch it? Paul tells Timothy to take hold of the eternal life to which he was called to. In other words, it's available, but Timothy must take hold of it. He does not automatically possess eternal life. It is not intrinsically his. Then, as if Paul wants to affirm for Timothy the certainty of every man's mortality, he attributes immortality to God alone. Even the wording is interesting. Paul says that God alone *has* immortality. Did he mean that only God has it and only God can give it? Perhaps he only means that God alone is immortal. Either way, it's clear that Paul is telling Timothy that neither he (Paul), Timothy, nor anyone else is immortal but God.

In his letter to the Romans, Paul, speaking of God's righteous judgment, pens this:

> *He will render to each one according to his works: to those who by patience in well-doing seek for glory and honor and immortality, he will give eternal life; but for those who are self-seeking and do not obey the truth, but obey unrighteousness, there will be wrath and fury. (Romans 2:6-8 ESV)*

On the day of judgment, God will give to each according to his works. Notice that immortality is something to be sought after, not something that we already have. If found righteous, then God will give eternal life. Otherwise, He won't.

Afterlife accounts

The Bible has at least ten accounts, both in the Old and New Testaments, about people being raised from the dead. In one account in the Book of 2 Kings, a dead man's body was thrown in the grave of Elisha, the prophet. When the dead body touched Elisha's bones, the man came to life. In the Book of Acts, a woman dies, and her friends go to get the apostle Peter, who was in a nearby town. Peter comes and with just two words, "*Tabitha, arise,*" brings the woman to life. The Bible says, "*and it became known throughout all Joppa, and many believed in the Lord*" *(Acts 9:36-42).* Perhaps the most famous of all the accounts is the story of Jesus raising Lazarus from the dead, four days after his passing, mentioned previously. One account even tells us of many people being raised from the dead at the same time. It is when Jesus dies on the cross. This is the account:

> *And Jesus cried out again with a loud voice and yielded up his spirit. And behold, the curtain of the temple was torn in two, from top to bottom. And the earth shook, and the rocks were split. The tombs also were opened. And many bodies of the saints who had fallen asleep were raised, and coming out of the tombs after his resurrection they went into the holy city and appeared to many. (Matthew 27:50-53 ESV)*

These and others are all stories of the great power of God and the hope that we have even after death. Yet there is one thing missing from every single one of these accounts: the telling of what they experienced while dead.

Lazarus was dead for four days, and there is not one word recorded of what he experienced while dead. Tabitha's story became known throughout all Joppa. We wonder how many people must have heard that story, and yet there is no account concerning her after-death experience. The account tells us that there were many of them and that they went into the holy city and appeared to many. One would think that their after-death experience would be of much talk and excitement, just as newsworthy as the actual resurrection event. Yet, in all of scripture, there isn't a single word about what any resurrected person experienced while dead. Could it be because there was nothing to tell?

Also, as in Paul's letter to the Thessalonians referenced previously, there is no mention of a reuniting of body and soul of any of these that came to life. This seems like a glaring omission.

Based on all these passages, we can conclude that no part of us is immortal and that there is no consciousness after death. Whatever we believe makes up a human being, it doesn't seem that any of it remains alive, or active, or conscious after we die.

SUMMARY

This chapter explores the question of what happens to individuals when they die.

- Debate About Afterlife: The chapter starts by acknowledging the longstanding debate about what happens when people die, both within and outside of religious contexts.

- The Concept of the Soul: It discusses the concept of the soul as something that potentially lives apart from the physical body after death, assuming it to be immortal.

- Popular Beliefs About Heaven: Many Christians believe that when a person dies, their soul goes to heaven, and even some non-Christians share this belief.

- Biblical Passages Examined: The chapter examines various biblical passages to shed light on what happens when people die, including passages from the books of John, Daniel, and the Psalms.

- The Last Day: It explores the concept of the "last day" as mentioned in the Bible and whether it implies an immediate departure to heaven after death.

- Letters from Paul: The chapter discusses passages from the letters of Paul, who is often cited as a source for the idea of an immediate afterlife in heaven. However, it notes that the one or two passages used to support this view are inconclusive. Instead, when examining all of Paul's writings, it becomes evident that his primary belief was in an afterlife that would occur at Jesus' second coming. Additionally, Paul emphasized that only God possesses immortality, implying that humans do not inherently possess immortality.

- No Consciousness After Death: The chapter presents several passages from the Bible that suggest there is no consciousness or awareness after death. It highlights verses where people who have died are described as being in a state of sleep or rest.

- Immortality of the Soul: The chapter questions the idea of the immortality of the soul and argues that the Bible supports the view that no part of a person remains conscious after death.

- Afterlife Accounts: It mentions biblical accounts of people being raised from the dead, such as Lazarus and the saints after Jesus' crucifixion, and notes that these accounts don't provide any details of their experiences during their time of death.

Conclusion

The chapter concludes that based on the examined biblical passages, there is no evidence to support the idea of an immortal soul or consciousness after death.

Questions for Reflection or Group Study Discussion

1. Did the passages and arguments presented in this chapter change your view on the topic? Why or why not?

2. What passages had you not previously considered regarding this topic?

3. If your understanding differed from what was presented in this chapter, how was it different, and how did you come to have that understanding?

4. Regardless of your final position on the topic (agree or disagree), did you learn anything new? If so, what?

PART 2

Where do we go When we Die?

(The Heaven Arguments)

Chapter Two

Contradictory Views on The Afterlife

Why are there so many people who think we go to heaven directly after dying and/or that our soul is somehow immortally conscious somewhere? The answer, of course, is because there are verses in the Bible that seem to say so; with emphasis on the word *seem*. In this next section, we will tackle a few of the major passages used in an attempt to make this case.

Argument 1: Rachel, the wife of Jacob

The first of these passages is found in Genesis. We read where Rachel, the wife of Jacob, dies as she is giving birth to their last child, Benjamin.

> *And as her soul was departing (for she was dying), she called his name Ben-oni; but his father called him Benjamin. (Genesis 35:18 ESV)*

Where was her soul departing to? We've already read in more than several passages that the dead have no consciousness. Where, then, is this soul with no consciousness going?

The key to unlocking this mystery is in understanding what the word *soul* actually means.

Consider these lines:
- A father guards his children with his **life**

- A mother loves her child with all her **being**

- True compassion is only found in the **person** of Jesus

The words *life*, *being*, and *person* are more conceptual than actual matter. You can't take someone's being and move it from one place to another. In the Hebrew language, these words are the word *nephesh*, which is the English word *soul*. If you were told that cancer took a friend's life, you would not ask where to. You understand that "life" has no physical nature per se that could be transported. It is the same with the word *soul* in the case of Rachel.

Let's confirm this with scripture and see some examples of how the word *soul* is used.

> *And the LORD God formed man of the dust of the ground, and breathed into his nostrils the breath*

of life; and man became a living soul. (Genesis 2:7 KJV)

Notice that God did not give man a soul, man became a living soul by the combining of dust and breath. To be more precise, the breath gave life to the body and in doing so, became a living soul. So, in short, we don't have a soul, we are a soul.

When God was giving instructions regarding how priests should maintain their holiness, He says this:

He must not enter a place where there is a dead body. He must not make himself unclean, even for his father or mother, (Leviticus 21:11 NIV)

The word *body* in this passage is the Hebrew word *nephesh* that we mentioned before, the word that means *soul*. When the priests heard that they should stay away from a dead soul, they were not envisioning some ghostly matter lying dead on the ground. They understood that the command was to stay away from a person who just died.

This tells us at least two things. The first is that body and soul are one, not two different things that can be pulled apart. The other is that there is no such thing as an immortal soul since, according to this passage, souls die.

After God delivered Israel from Egypt, He gave them many commands. Here are a couple of them in the King James version of the Bible:

Seven days shall ye eat unleavened bread; even the first day ye shall put away leaven out of your

> houses: *for whosoever eateth leavened bread from the first day until the seventh day, that **soul** shall be cut off from Israel. (Exodus 12:15 KJV)*

> *Or if a **soul** touch any unclean thing, whether it be a carcase of an unclean beast, or a carcase of unclean cattle, or the carcase of unclean creeping things, and if it be hidden from him; he also shall be unclean, and guilty. (Leviticus 5:2 KJV)*

> *And if any **soul** sin through ignorance, then he shall bring a she goat of the first year for a sin offering. (Numbers 15:27 KJV)*

When we look at these verses in other Bible translations, we see that the word *soul* is swapped out for the word *person*. There are over 400 instances of the word *soul* being used in a similar fashion in the Bible and many times translated as *person, creature, life,* or *being*. Why? Because that's its basic meaning.

Remember our question — where does a person go when they die? Even though *person* and *soul* are synonymous, we would never say something like "his person lives on," we say, "his soul lives on." Do you see the mental contradiction? If we can say, "The person in the passenger seat died," then we can say, "The soul in the passenger seat died." And if the soul in the passenger seat died, then the soul is not immortal — no more than a person is immortal.

With that in mind, let's examine one more verse. Here, God is speaking to Noah after the flood, giving him his marching orders and commands. When speaking about taking the life of another, God says this:

> *And surely your blood of your lives will I require; at the hand of every beast will I require it, and at the hand of man; at the hand of every man's brother will I require the life of man. (Genesis 9:5 KJV)*

God is saying, he who takes a life, their life He will take. The words *lives* and *life* in this verse are both the Hebrew word *nephesh*. The word *soul*. Therefore, we can take a statement such as, "In the accident, the driver lost his life." and convert it to its Biblical form, "In the accident, the driver lost his soul." Both mean that the driver died.

Putting this all together, we can now understand Genesis 35:18 as intended. Saying that Rachel's *soul was departing* is the same as saying that *her life was departing*.

To make sure that we are not overstepping boundaries in our interpretation, let's look at this verse again and in two other Bible translations.

> *And as her soul was departing (for she was dying), she called his name Ben-oni; but his father called him Benjamin. (Genesis 35:18 ESV)*

> *With her dying breath, she named him Ben Oni. But his father called him Benjamin instead. (Genesis 35:18 NET)*

> *As she breathed her last—for she was dying—she named her son Ben-Oni. But his father named him Benjamin. (Genesis 35:18 NIV)*

As we can see, Genesis 35:18 is not saying that some element of Rachel was leaving her body and heading somewhere. This verse is simply letting us know that Rachel was dying.

With this new understanding, we can see that this verse would be a poor verse choice to argue that when we die, there is a conscious part of us on its way to heaven.

Argument 2: The thief on the cross

In Luke's account of the crucifixion, one of the two men crucified alongside Jesus makes an appeal for Jesus to remember him when He comes into His kingdom. This is how Jesus responds:

> *And he said to him, "Truly, I say to you, today you will be with me in paradise." (Luke 23:43 ESV)*

Many argue that this is proof that when we die, we go directly to heaven. Right off the bat, we need to ask, is the word *paradise* here referring to heaven? To answer that, we should look at other verses in the Bible where the word *paradise* is found and see how it is used.

The word *paradise* appears in the Bible only three times. The second place we find it in is in one of the letters to the Corinthians, where Paul is recounting an experience that he had years prior.

> *I know a man in Christ who fourteen years ago was caught up to the third heaven—whether in the body or out of the body I do not know, God knows. And I know that this man was caught up into paradise—whether in the body or out of the body I do not know, God knows— and he heard things that cannot be told, which man may not utter. (2 Corinthians 12:2-4 ESV)*

Traditionally it is said that there are three heavens. The first is where the clouds are and where the birds fly. The second is where the moon, sun, and stars sit. And the third is where the angels and God dwell.

It appears that Paul is calling the third heaven, paradise. However, if paradise is heaven, then we have a problem because Jesus tells the man that he's going to be with Him in paradise that very day, the day they both died, but Jesus did not ascend to heaven until days later. In the Book of John, we read Mary Magdalene's encounter with Jesus after His resurrection, which took place on the third day after His death.

> *Jesus said to her, "Do not cling to me, for I have not yet ascended to the Father; but go to my brothers and say to them, 'I am ascending to my Father and your Father, to my God and your God.'" (John 20:17 ESV)*

We see that even as of day three, Jesus had not yet ascended to the Father. One might argue that although the text says that

He didn't ascend to the Father, it doesn't say that He didn't ascend to heaven. Although that would be to say that Jesus went to heaven but didn't bother to check in with the Father, and that seems unlikely.

How, then, do we reconcile Jesus telling the man that he would be with Him in paradise on that day when, in fact, Jesus did not ascend to heaven until the third day? Did Jesus lie to the man, or did they go somewhere else, which Jesus refers to as paradise, but which is not heaven, the dwelling place of God? We can only speculate on the matter of what or where paradise is that Jesus refers to here. What we do know is that Jesus did not ascend to heaven till the third day. To say that the thief went to heaven with Jesus the day they died would be doing so with no real evidence or supporting scripture.

Here is the third place where the word *paradise* is seen:

> *He who has an ear, let him hear what the Spirit says to the churches. To the one who conquers I will grant to eat of the tree of life, which is in the paradise of God. (Revelation 2:7 ESV)*

As seen here, those who conquer are granted to eat from the Tree of Life, which is in the paradise of God. Where exactly is this paradise that is mentioned here? If paradise is in heaven, when did God move the Tree of Life? Isn't the Tree of Life in the Garden of Eden, which is somewhere on Earth?

In these two verses below, we see where God put the Tree of Life during creation and how He had it guarded after He drove Adam out.

> *And out of the ground the LORD God made to spring up every tree that is pleasant to the sight and good for food. The tree of life was in the midst of the garden, and the tree of the knowledge of good and evil. (Genesis 2:9 ESV)*

> *He drove out the man, and at the east of the garden of Eden he placed the cherubim and a flaming sword that turned every way to guard the way to the tree of life. (Genesis 3:24 ESV)*

So, God put the Tree of Life in the Garden of Eden, which He created on Earth. When Adam and Eve sinned and were banished from the garden, God put cherubim to guard the way to the Tree of Life. There is no account in the Bible that tells us that God moved the tree.

One might argue that the Tree of Life referenced here is not the same Tree of Life referenced in Genesis. This argument might arise from reading Revelation 22 where it speaks of the Tree of Life significantly "greater" than the Tree of Life in the Garden of Eden. Yet the argument would be of no consequence since the Tree of Life spoken of in Revelation 22 resides within the new earth and not heaven.

As unsettling for our interpretation as it might sound, it appears that paradise is a different place in all three of the only three accounts found in the Bible. In Luke's account, it is a place where the man crucified with Jesus wound up when he died (not heaven). In Paul's account (Corinthians), it is in the heavens above. In John's account (Revelation), it is where the Tree of Life is planted, which, as far as we know, is in the

Garden of Eden on Earth somewhere (current Earth or new Earth).

To add more fuel to this fire, while the word *paradise* is found only three times in the English-translated Bible and only in the New Testament, the Hebrew word for it also appears three times in the Old Testament. In Nehemiah 2:8, it is translated as *forest*. In Ecclesiastes 2:5 and Song of Solomon 4:13, it is translated as *orchard* or *park*. None of which are heaven.

It is worth noting that much has been written concerning the word *paradise* in extra-Biblical accounts. Opinions differ, but there seems to be a common theme that paradise is the resting place of the righteous or blessed; it is not, however, heaven. Whether there is consciousness or not is just as commonly debated. Considering all of the scripture that we have gone through here, it doesn't seem likely that there is consciousness.

Can we say then that the word *paradise*, as seen in Luke's account, is referring to heaven? It's difficult to see how. Not by the accounts in the Bible, and from this author's research, less so by extra-Biblical accounts.

Our final point concerns another popular view concerning Jesus' words to the man crucified next to Him. It is the idea that a comma has been placed incorrectly. The argument is that the comma before the word *today* should actually be after it. So, instead of *"Truly, I say to you, today you will be with me in paradise,"* it should read, *"Truly, I say to you today, you will be with me in paradise."*

In this view, all arguments would come to a halt since Jesus' words promise that the thief would be with Him in paradise, but not necessarily on that day. This interpretation is completely in accordance with the whole of the gospel and the actual account of the crucifixion day and the days that followed prior to Jesus ascending to the Father.

Whatever view one might subscribe to, the outcome of our discussion here is the same: the account of the thief on the cross does not support the idea that when we die, we go directly to heaven or that a dead person or soul (which is the same as saying person) has any consciousness.

Argument 3: Paul's Letter to the Philippians

At the time of the writing of the letter to the Philippians, the apostle Paul was in jail. He explains that his imprisonment had served to advance the gospel and gives a couple of examples as to how, and for that, he rejoices. He hopes that in life or death, Christ will be honored. He then says these words:

> *For to me to live is Christ, and to die is gain. If I am to live in the flesh, that means fruitful labor for me. Yet which I shall choose I cannot tell. I am hard pressed between the two. My desire is to depart and be with Christ, for that is far better. But to remain in the flesh is more necessary on your account. (Philippians 1:21-23 ESV)*

Before we tackle this verse, let us keep in mind that this is Paul speaking. The same person who has told us in prior verses that immortality belongs to God only.

Paul says that between life and death, he considers death to be better because he would be with Christ. Some interpret this to mean that Paul believed that when he died, he would immediately go to be with Christ. Some further conclude that he believed that he would have consciousness after death. The reasoning is that Paul is comparing the benefits between life and death. If he thought that when he died, he was just going to sleep in the grave until the return of Christ, he probably would not have counted that as a benefit. His death would only be beneficial if he knew he was going to be with Christ at that very moment. Or so is the reasoning of some.

This sounds reasonable except for the fact that there are way too many other passages in the Bible that speak differently about what happens after death, as we have already covered, some of which are Paul's own writings. How else, then, can we interpret Paul's words? There are at least two things that we must consider. First, is the word *better*. Why would being dead with Christ be better than being alive? What did Paul think he would be doing once dead that would be better than what he was doing while alive on Earth? Keep in mind that Paul knows that the promise of eternal life, the new Heaven and Earth, doesn't happen until Jesus returns in the second coming. Does Paul know something that no one else knows about what goes on in death between now and Jesus' return? This leads us to the second point, which is an extension of this one.

Let us consider Paul's description of what staying alive would mean vs. what going to be with Christ would mean. He says that staying alive would result in fruitful labor. Yet he says nothing about what his death would result in. In this, he is silent. Paul says, *"If I am to live in the flesh, that means fruitful labor for me. Yet which I shall choose I cannot tell."* Shouldn't there be a statement between those two sentences comparing being alive to being dead? Perhaps something that says, *"If I am dead, that means rewards, and worship, and joy."* Yet he mentions nothing of the sort. In fact, in all his writings, we find nothing even remotely like that. Whenever Paul speaks about being with Christ after death, there is no mention of how time will be spent, not a single word.

Could it be, perhaps, that given his circumstances (jail and his many hardships) he was saying that he would be better off at rest, not having to further suffer what he was suffering? The truth is that we don't know for sure — no one knows. Paul does not give us a comparative view to help us understand why he thought it would be better to be with Christ other than to simply be joined to Him — and in what capacity or when he does not say. In other words, this passage gives us no definitive answer about when Paul thought he would be joined to Christ, so it does not make for a good argument since we would just be guessing. It would be careless and unwise to use these verses as evidence for this argument, given their weakness in support of it.

That's not to say that Paul does not answer the question of when we are gathered to Christ. In fact, he tackles the question head-on for the Thessalonians.

> *Now concerning the coming of our Lord Jesus Christ and our being gathered together to him, we ask you, brothers, not to be quickly shaken in mind or alarmed, either by a spirit or a spoken word, or a letter seeming to be from us, to the effect that the day of the Lord has come. Let no one deceive you in any way. For that day will not come, unless the rebellion comes first, and the man of lawlessness is revealed, the son of destruction, (2 Thessalonians 2:1-3)*

I don't think it can get clearer than this. Paul is teaching that we won't be gathered to Christ until His second coming, and that's not going to happen before the man of lawlessness is revealed, which has not yet happened. Considering the clarity of these verses compared to those in the letter to the Philippians, we are persuaded to lean on these instead.

Argument 4: Paul's letter to the Corinthians

Here we have another letter from Paul. This one is to the Corinthians.

> *For we know that if the tent that is our earthly home is destroyed, we have a building from God, a house not made with hands, eternal in the heavens. For in this tent we groan, longing to put on our heavenly dwelling, if indeed by putting it on we may not be found naked. For while we are still in this tent, we groan, being burdened—not that we would be unclothed, but that we would be further clothed, so that what is mortal may be swallowed up by life. He who has prepared us for this very thing is God, who has given us the Spirit as a guarantee. So we are always of good courage. We know that while we are at home in the body we are away from the Lord, for we walk by faith, not by sight. Yes, we are of good courage, and we would rather be away from the body and at home with the Lord. So whether we are at home or away, we make it our aim to please him. (2 Corinthians 5:1-9 ESV)*

Somewhat like in the letter to the Philippians, here Paul says, "*we would rather be away from the body and at home with the Lord.*" This similarity is important because this is one of the ways we build a case for any interpretation; we find other passages that support whatever hypothesis we are trying to argue for to ensure that our interpretation is not rogue.

But does this passage say the same thing that the Philippians letter says? The phrase, "*We would rather be away from the body and at home with the Lord,*" sounds suspiciously like what he says in the Philippians letter, "*My desire is to depart and be with Christ, for that is far better.*" Yet, if that's all we read, that's all we get.

Upon careful inspection of the full passage, we realize that it really says something quite different. In fact, it argues against the idea that there is a conscious version of us after death without a body.

The first four verses are quite telling regarding Paul's understanding of our existence. It appears that to Paul, an earthly life and a spiritual life both require a body, "*For we know that if the tent that is our earthly home is destroyed, we have a building from God.*" He says that in our mortal body, we groan as if it were uncomfortable, wanting something better. Not that we want to do away with the mortal body and be left with nothing (unclothed), but that we rather be clothed with the heavenly dwelling. In Paul's mind, being unclothed (without a body) is not an option. In other words, to have any existence, we need a body.

Also, once again, we see Paul speaking about death with no mention whatsoever of a conscious soul that is somehow separate from a body.

Now, is Paul saying that we go from mortal body to spiritual body the moment we die? No. Not at all. We know this because we know that Paul believes that the resurrection of the dead happens later, at Jesus' second coming, which is when we get that new body. We can see that mindset in his letter to Timothy:

> *But avoid irreverent babble, for it will lead people into more and more ungodliness, and their talk will spread like gangrene. Among them are Hymenaeus and Philetus, who have swerved from the truth, saying that the resurrection has already happened. They are upsetting the faith of some. (2 Timothy 2:16-18 ESV)*

Another thing to consider is that if we assume that Paul is saying that immediately after dying, we go straight to be with the Lord, and knowing that should bring us good courage, then what need is there for the resurrection, which he himself argues for? If the desired goal is to leave the body to be immediately joined to Jesus, and that is achieved the moment we die, then it sounds like there is nothing else to be done. We can skip the whole resurrection thing since we have achieved our goal.

This, too, once read in context, would be a poor choice to argue for an immortal soul or consciousness after death.

Argument 4 Cont.: Does Paul disagree with Peter and John?

To say that Paul believed that the soul is immortal and has consciousness after death would be to say that Paul and Peter did not agree on this issue. At Pentecost, after Jesus' death, resurrection, and ascension, Peter preached his first sermon. This is the account of when the tongues of fire came on the disciples in the upper room, found in the Book of Acts. In this sermon, Peter brings up a Psalm written by King David and refers to this verse:

> *For you will not abandon my soul to Sheol, or let your holy one see corruption. (Psalm 16:10 ESV)*

There are two very specific things that Peter was pointing out in this verse, which David himself was referring to. The first concerns the soul (*nephesh*), his being. David was saying that at death, his soul would not stay in the grave. The second concerns the body, saying that God would not allow it to eventually turn to dust.

Peter then tells the people that David was speaking prophetically. That he was not speaking about himself but about the Messiah. He makes this point with these words:

> *Brothers, I may say to you with confidence about the patriarch David that he both died and was buried, and his tomb is with us to this day. (Acts 2:29 ESV)*

> *he foresaw and spoke about the resurrection of the Christ, that he was not abandoned to Hades, nor did his flesh see corruption. (Acts 2:31 ESV)*

THAT'S NOT WHAT THE BIBLE SAYS

> *For David did not ascend into the heavens... (Acts 2:34 ESV)*

We've already established that the soul is simply one's life or being, but just in case you missed it, notice that although Peter is speaking of soul and body, in verse 31 the English Standard Version (ESV) uses the word *he* instead of *soul*, "*he was not abandoned to Hades.*" The NASB renders it the same way, while the New King James Bible uses the word *soul*. But we digress.

Peter is reminding his audience that death is equal to the abandonment of the soul (our being) in the grave and the body turning to dust. Peter is not trying to convince his audience that this is how death works; they already know that is how it works. He is simply pointing out that what David said would not happen to him did happen. David was abandoned to the grave (in other words, he didn't go anywhere beyond that), and his body did turn to dust. Peter says this in comparison to Jesus, who was not abandoned to the grave and whose body did not turn to dust.

The most important point that Peter wants to make is in verse 34. He makes it crystal clear that David did not ascend into heaven, and when he says "*David*" he means David's soul, *nephesh*, his being.

At Antioch in Pisidia, Paul makes the exact same point as Peter without variation.

> *Therefore he says also in another psalm, "'You will not let your Holy One see corruption.' For David, after he had served the purpose of God in his own*

> *generation, fell asleep and was laid with his fathers and saw corruption, but he whom God raised up did not see corruption. (Acts 13:35-37 ESV)*

Paul says that David fell asleep, was laid to rest, and saw corruption. There is no distinction between body and soul, *he* (David) saw corruption. There is no indication whatsoever that Paul thinks that David's body saw corruption, but another part of him went somewhere else. Because if Paul thought that David was immortally enjoying himself in heaven, wouldn't making this point here be moot since technically David would be just as well off as Jesus?

It is Peter's specific objective, as is Paul's, to let his audience know that in the history of mankind, only Jesus has made it out of the grave and has ascended into heaven after death.

The apostle John records that Jesus agrees with Peter. In John's gospel, Jesus tells us that only one person has ever ascended into heaven. Do you want to guess who that might be?

> *No one has ascended into heaven except he who descended from heaven, the Son of Man. (John 3:13 ESV)*

Considering this, we might want to return to Paul's letter to the Philippians and ask the question again, was Paul really saying that right after death, his immortal soul would be going to heaven to be with Jesus in some conscious state? Because if he did, he would be in total disagreement with Peter and Jesus.

Argument 5: Lazarus and the rich man

There is another character in the Bible named Lazarus. He is not the same Lazarus that Jesus resurrected after being dead for four days. This Lazarus was a poor beggar whose life is contrasted with that of a rich man.

Some people argue that the account of Lazarus and the rich man, found in Luke 16, is a factual story and not a parable. Thereby being an example of the dead having consciousness. One argument for saying that this story was a true account is that Jesus never used names in His parables, so this must be a real account. While that might be a good place to start to build a case, it cannot be the only evidence. We can just as easily, using the same logic, argue the opposite thing. We can argue that Jesus never told stories like this one that were factual. Every single recorded "story" that Jesus told was a parable, so this one too must be a parable. One way or the other, there must be more evidence to help us get to a sound conclusion. Let us review the account:

> *There was a rich man who was clothed in purple and fine linen and who feasted sumptuously every day. And at his gate was laid a poor man named Lazarus, covered with sores, who desired to be fed with what fell from the rich man's table. Moreover, even the dogs came and licked his sores.*
>
> *The poor man died and was carried by the angels to Abraham's side. The rich man also died and was buried, and in Hades, being in torment, he*

lifted up his eyes and saw Abraham far off and Lazarus at his side.

And he called out, 'Father Abraham, have mercy on me, and send Lazarus to dip the end of his finger in water and cool my tongue, for I am in anguish in this flame.' But Abraham said, 'Child, remember that you in your lifetime received your good things, and Lazarus in like manner bad things; but now he is comforted here, and you are in anguish.

And besides all this, between us and you a great chasm has been fixed, in order that those who would pass from here to you may not be able, and none may cross from there to us.'

And he said, 'Then I beg you, father, to send him to my father's house— for I have five brothers—so that he may warn them, lest they also come into this place of torment.'

But Abraham said, 'They have Moses and the Prophets; let them hear them.'

And he said, 'No, father Abraham, but if someone goes to them from the dead, they will repent.'

He said to him, 'If they do not hear Moses and the Prophets, neither will they be convinced if someone should rise from the dead.'" (Luke 16:19-31 ESV)

If this was a true account, then it would be difficult to argue that the dead don't have consciousness. If it turns out that it is a parable instead, then we can move on to other arguments.

Let us begin with the fact that both the rich man and Lazarus have functioning bodies in this story. That alone should be enough proof that it is not a true account. If nothing else, we know that we don't get our new heavenly bodies until the resurrection (see Paul's letters to the Corinthians), yet the rich man is asking Abraham to let Lazarus dip his finger in water to cool the rich man's tongue — evidence that in this story, they all have functioning bodies. Where did they get these bodies from?

In the King James version of the Bible and others, instead of Lazarus being taken to Abraham's side, it says, "Abraham's bosom." Nowhere else in the Christian Bible does the phrase "Abraham's bosom" appear. Those who believe that when we die, we go directly to heaven, say that the term refers to heaven. But is that what the audience had in mind when they heard those words? Not likely.

Whether it is Abraham's bosom or side, to the Jew, this phrase would have painted a very specific picture of the coming kingdom. In one of the books of Maccabee, which appears in some manuscripts of the Septuagint, we find this verse:

> *For if we so die, Abraham and Isaac and Jacob will welcome us, and all the fathers will praise us. (4 Maccabee 13:17 NRSV)*

The idea is that the righteous people of God, those who do not transgress His commandments, have a promise of being welcomed into the kingdom by Abraham, Isaac, and Jacob. Jesus Himself refers to this idea as well:

> *When Jesus heard this, he marveled and said to those who followed him, "Truly, I tell you, with no one in Israel have I found such faith. I tell you, many will come from east and west and recline at table with Abraham, Isaac, and Jacob in the kingdom of heaven, while the sons of the kingdom will be thrown into the outer darkness. In that place there will be weeping and gnashing of teeth." (Matthew 8:10-12 ESV)*

The concept of Abraham's bosom or side would not have been a picture of heaven but of a future kingdom.

Let us now turn to logical thinking. (Yes, we should be reading God's word with spiritual eyes, but that doesn't mean that we ignore that which is logical.) In this account, we have the rich man in Hades (the place of the dead) speaking to Lazarus the beggar who is in . . . where exactly?

Well, let's consider that they are close enough to see each other and hear each other when they speak. If this is a real story depicting actual physical places, this is going to be a real problem. Can we imagine an existence where family members are on opposite sides of this great chasm, as the rich man and Lazarus are painted here? Those saved to Abraham's side watching their loved ones in anguish in flames while able to hear their cries. Logically, this can't be a real place. At least not in the way it is being depicted.

Finally, how about some context? Upon inspecting the complete chapter, we can see that Jesus is talking about money.

There are two major sections that precede this one. The first is referred to as the Parable of the Dishonest Manager. It is a teaching about how we should use our money. The second section, which starts in verse 14, tells us that those listening were Pharisees who were lovers of money and were scoffing at what Jesus was saying. This tells us that the focus of the story of the rich man and Lazarus is money, not after-life matters, and specifically aimed directly at these money-loving listeners. It is the perfect setting for a parable — and so very similar to the setting of the many other parables that Jesus told.

What about the twist in giving Lazarus a name since Jesus never used names in his parables? Perhaps it's not as mysterious as we might think. We said that verse 14 tells us that the Pharisees were scoffing at Jesus. In verse 15, Jesus says that they were men who sought to justify themselves. We get a picture of proud men of means, sneering in their confidence. That's who Jesus was speaking to. Now, let us consider how a listener was supposed to decipher a parable. They were supposed to figure out which character in the parable represented them. That's why none of the characters in Jesus' parables have names; one is supposed to find oneself in the story. But by Jesus giving Lazarus a name, He ruled out the beggar as one of the characters available for anyone to relate to. No one listening could say that the beggar in the story represented them since the beggar had a specific name. Likewise, Abraham is mentioned by name, and so the character of the man who welcomes the beggar is also not up for grabs. The only character without a name is the rich man. By default, everyone listening is the rich man. Of course, there is no Biblical evidence for this last argument here, and I present it for your consideration as my personal observation of how Jesus' parables are laid out.

Even if we reject the name explanation just mentioned, we simply cannot ignore the last three verses which are dripping with parabolic language and references.

> *But Abraham said, 'They have Moses and the Prophets; let them hear them.' And he said, 'No, father Abraham, but if someone goes to them from the dead, they will repent.' He said to him, 'If they do not hear Moses and the Prophets, neither will they be convinced if someone should rise from the dead.' (Luke 16:29-31 ESV)*

Notice that another character is introduced. Someone who comes back from the dead. We might be tempted to think this is referring to Lazarus but from the word exchange, it seems a bit obvious that it is not. For the entire story, Lazarus' name is used by both the rich man and Abraham, then suddenly, it isn't. Suddenly, it's just a certain *someone*. Of course, that someone would be Jesus.

Jesus is saying that the rich man and his brothers (i.e., the listeners) have already been warned by their own scriptures, but their hardened hearts rejected that which they've been taught since their youth. And if a lifetime of teaching has not turned them, even someone (Jesus) coming back from the dead would not convince them.

In short, there is enough evidence to conclude that this story is a parable and not a real account. Because of this, it cannot be used to argue that when we die, we go to heaven and/or have consciousness.

Argument 6: God of the living

Three of the gospels record Jesus responding to some Sadducees who came to Him with a hypothetical situation concerning the resurrection. His response to them ends like this:

> *And as for the dead being raised, have you not read in the book of Moses, in the passage about the bush, how God spoke to him, saying, 'I am the God of Abraham, and the God of Isaac, and the God of Jacob'? He is not God of the dead, but of the living. You are quite wrong. (Mark 12:26-27 ESV)*

The common interpretation of this is that the soul is still alive after the body has died because God Himself said that He is not God of the dead but of the living, and to be God of the living, something must be alive. If God said that He is the God of Abraham, Isaac, and Jacob, and He is God of the living only, then these men must somehow, in some fashion, still be alive.

The logic is sound, but is that what Jesus was saying? To know, we need to get a better picture of the setting, the audience, and the conversation in which these words were injected.

The audience is a group of Sadducees. The Bible tells us that the Sadducees were a sect in the same way that the Pharisees were a sect. The Sadducees did not believe in the resurrection, and that is how this account begins — telling us that they are not believers of the resurrection. This would be our first clue that the resurrection has something to do with, or perhaps everything to do with, why Jesus responds the way He does.

They pose the question to Jesus as a hypothetical situation. The idea seems to be that if the resurrection was a real thing, it would prove to be problematic. This hypothetical situation is supposed to expose that problem. This is how they ask it:

> *And Sadducees came to him, who say that there is no resurrection. And they asked him a question, saying, "Teacher, Moses wrote for us that if a man's brother dies and leaves a wife, but leaves no child, the man must take the widow and raise up offspring for his brother. There were seven brothers; the first took a wife, and when he died left no offspring. And the second took her, and died, leaving no offspring. And the third likewise. And the seven left no offspring. Last of all the woman also died. In the resurrection, when they rise again, whose wife will she be? For the seven had her as wife." (Mark 12:18-23 ESV)*

It's quite clever, actually. Perhaps we should do more of this kind of processing when we read scripture and ask these "what if" questions since quite often it leads us to uncover the malice in our original assumptions.

Anyways, this is Jesus' full response, including our two verses:

> *Jesus said to them, "Is this not the reason you are wrong, because you know neither the Scriptures nor the power of God? For when they rise from the dead, they neither marry nor are given in mar-*

> *riage, but are like angels in heaven. And as for the dead being raised, have you not read in the book of Moses, in the passage about the bush, how God spoke to him, saying, 'I am the God of Abraham, and the God of Isaac, and the God of Jacob'? He is not God of the dead, but of the living. You are quite wrong." (Mark 12:24-27 ESV)*

Jesus' answer is quite simple. He tells them that in the resurrection, the concept of marriage does not exist. At this point, the conversation should be over, the question has been asked and answered. But then Jesus makes another statement, the one that we started this section with, telling them that God is God of the living, not the dead. So, what does God being God of the living have to do with the question they asked? Absolutely nothing. Actually, that's not entirely true. Jesus knows that they are asking the question because they don't believe in the resurrection. It seems that He wants to not only answer their original question but also tackle their underlying misconception.

The point Jesus seems to be making to the Sadducees is that if they knew scripture, they would have noticed that God said, "I am" the God of Abraham, Isaac, and Jacob, not "I was." He wants them to consider how God could make that statement in the present tense when Abraham had been dead for over 300 years when He made it.

This is where the argument could go either way. One could argue that Jesus was pointing out that the souls of these three men were still alive, and that's why God made the statement in the present tense. However, to come to that conclusion would be to ignore what this conversation is actually about and ignore how Jesus began His argument.

The conversation is not about souls still being alive, it is about whether the resurrection (a future thing) is a real thing. And when Jesus begins to answer them, He says that they are wrong in their presupposition because they don't know scripture or the power of God. We must anticipate then that Jesus is going to point out how their knowledge of scripture and God's power is flawed. We must necessarily look for that in the text.

By directing them to this Old Testament conversation between God and Moses, Jesus tackles both issues and forces them to consider the implications of God's words. By God making a statement in the present tense about men known to be long dead, He essentially declares His power over time and death. Such is His power. So powerful that He can speak of the dead as if they were still alive, knowing that He could resurrect them at any moment if He so wished to do. Thereby also proving that the resurrection must be real, for if God was not planning to resurrect His people, He would not have spoken as if He already had. In other words, God's statement could only be true if He had already deemed that it would be so, making the resurrection a necessary reality.

If you are a deep thinker, and I sincerely hope you are, especially as you read this book, then you may not be 100% satisfied. As complete as this explanation might be, and as much sense as it might make, it is technically missing one thing: other scripture to support it. Wouldn't it be nice to have that last piece of the pie?

As it turns out, this one is quite easy. As mentioned in the beginning, this account is captured in three of the four gospels.

We simply need to turn to Luke's account and see how he pens Jesus' last statement in His response.

> *Now he is not God of the dead, but of the living, <u>for all live to him</u>. (Luke 20:38 ESV)*

Those last four words confirm what we've discussed. God can speak of the dead as if they were alive because, to Him, they are.

The idea that the dead are alive in God's mind, shows us that God's reality is not bound by situation, time, or space. Only He can claim with absolute certainty that what will be already is because He not only deems it but also makes it so. If that doesn't show us God's power, I don't know what does.

This should not surprise us since the idea that what is dead can also be said to be alive is not foreign to us. If you have been a Christian for more than five minutes, then you are very familiar with this concept and have probably recited it a thousand times. It's that statement that we make of what our lives were before coming to know Christ; "we were dead in our trespasses." We can say that a person without Christ, although in effect alive, is dead because that is the true condition of their fate in the Father's eyes.

Another example of this concept is found in the parable of the lost son, or the prodigal son as most know it. In this parable, the youngest son dishonors his father and leaves for a foreign country. He then loses all his wealth and comes back home penniless. Ultimately, the father forgives him and throws a party to celebrate his return. The oldest son, however, is furious and refuses to celebrate. The father reasons with the oldest son, saying these words:

> *It was fitting to celebrate and be glad, for this your brother was dead, and is alive; he was lost, and is found. (Luke 15:32 ESV)*

Was the younger brother really dead? Of course not. But to the family, in his absence and absolute rebellion, he was dead.

In summary, this passage in Mark 12 does not support the idea that when we die, we ascend to heaven, that our souls are immortal, or that we have any consciousness after death.

Argument 7: Body and soul reunited

Let us tackle one last argument. There is a very detailed story in the Bible of a full-blown step-by-step resurrection that gives us more cause to dismiss the body-soul-reunion concept altogether. The account is found in the Old Testament in the Book of Ezekiel.

This is the account known as The Valley of Dry Bones. The prophet Ezekiel has a vision of being in a valley surrounded by dry human bones. God asks Ezekiel if he thinks the bones can come to life, but Ezekiel does not know. God tells him to prophecy over the bones that they may live. Ezekiel does so, and the bones start to rattle and move toward each other, coming together bone to bone. But even after they came together, the bodies were still dead. The account continues like this:

> *And I looked, and behold, there were sinews on them, and flesh had come upon them, and skin had covered them. But there was no breath in*

> *them. Then he said to me, "Prophesy to the breath; prophesy, son of man, and say to the breath, Thus says the Lord GOD: Come from the four winds, O breath, and breathe on these slain, that they may live." So I prophesied as he commanded me, and the breath came into them, and they lived and stood on their feet, an exceedingly great army. (Ezekiel 37:8-10 ESV)*

It's a chilling account. It must have been an incredible vision. What is conspicuously missing is the mention of souls. There is nothing whatsoever about souls reuniting with bodies. What it does mention is what we already knew, what we've already read, and which is completely in line with how God made Adam; dead bodies come to life by receiving breath, not souls.

Hopefully, the evidence here has been enough to put the idea of immortal souls to rest. But if for some reason there is still doubt about the meaning of the word *soul* or its fate compared to the body, then listen to God's words to Ezekiel.

> *Behold, all souls are mine; the soul of the father as well as the soul of the son is mine: the soul who sins shall die. (Ezekiel 18:4 ESV)*

So, whether you have learned that the soul is simply a person's being or believe that it is a separate thing from the body, it really doesn't matter because, according to God, souls die.

Exceptions

I think it is difficult for some people to think that God may have exceptions. As if being perfect means no exceptions. That thinking makes it harder for us to reconcile passages in scripture that seem to contradict themselves. And perhaps *"exceptions"* is not even the right terminology. Perhaps it's the idea that God can accomplish His plans by different means even when they seem contradictory to how He has done something similar in the past.

A case in point are the accounts of Enoch and Elijah.

> *Enoch walked with God, and he was not, for God took him. (Genesis 5:24 ESV)*

> *By faith Enoch was taken up so that he should not see death, and he was not found, because God had taken him. Now before he was taken he was commended as having pleased God. (Hebrews 11:5 ESV)*

> *And as they still went on and talked, behold, chariots of fire and horses of fire separated the two of them. And Elijah went up by a whirlwind into heaven. (2 Kings 2:11 ESV)*

Where exactly did God take Enoch? Was it heaven, as He did with Elijah? While that would be a great study, it is of little consequence for our current topic since neither of these men ever saw death. We cannot use these passages to prove that when we die (which they didn't), we go to heaven. If anything, it says that only living beings exist in heaven.

SUMMARY

This chapter critically examines common arguments used to support the belief in an immortal soul or immediate heavenly existence after death. The seven main arguments examined are:

Argument 1: Rachel, the wife of Jacob

The chapter discusses the story of Rachel's death in Genesis 35:18, where her "soul was departing" as she died. The argument presented revolves around the interpretation of the term "soul" (nephesh in Hebrew) and suggests that it does not refer to an immortal, conscious entity but rather to the essence of life itself. This view posits that humans do not possess immortal souls but are themselves living souls. Therefore, when Rachel's soul departed, it was a way of saying that her life was ending rather than her soul moving to another realm.

Argument 2: The thief on the cross

The chapter examines Luke 23:43, where Jesus tells the thief on the cross, "Truly, I say to you, today you will be with me in paradise." The argument here centers on the interpretation of "paradise" and suggests that it may not necessarily mean heaven as commonly believed. The chapter raises questions about the timing of this event, emphasizing that Jesus did not ascend to heaven until days later, which challenges the idea that the thief went to heaven immediately upon death.

Argument 3: Paul's Letter to the Philippians

In Philippians 1:21-23, Paul expresses his desire to depart and be with Christ, which some interpret as evidence that he believed in an immediate heavenly afterlife. The chapter examines this passage and argues that it does not conclusively support the idea of immediate consciousness after death. It suggests that Paul's words may be understood as expressing a desire for rest or relief from suffering rather than implying immediate conscious existence in heaven.

Argument 4: Paul's Letter to the Corinthians

The chapter discusses 2 Corinthians 5:1-9, where Paul speaks about the earthly tent and the heavenly dwelling. While some may interpret this passage as evidence of immediate heavenly existence after death, the chapter presents an alternative interpretation. It argues that Paul's focus is on the transformation from mortality to immortality, which occurs at the resurrection, rather than at the moment of death. The chapter emphasizes that Paul's writings consistently point to the resurrection as the time when believers will be reunited with Christ.

Argument 5: Lazarus and the Rich Man

In Luke 16:19-31, Jesus tells the story of Lazarus, a poor beggar, and a rich man. Some argue that this account is a factual story rather than a parable, suggesting that it demonstrates the consciousness of the dead. However, several factors suggest that it is a parable:

- Both Lazarus and the rich man have functioning bodies in the story, which contradicts the biblical teaching that resurrected bodies are received in the future.
- The term "Abraham's bosom" referred to a future kingdom, not heaven, in Jewish understanding.
- Logically, the story's portrayal of the rich man and Lazarus separated by a chasm raises questions about the nature of the afterlife.
- The context of the chapter focuses on money, suggesting that this is a parable about wealth rather than the afterlife.

Argument 6: God of the Living

In Mark 12:26-27, Jesus responds to the Sadducees' question about the resurrection by referring to God as the God of Abraham, Isaac, and Jacob, implying that these patriarchs are still alive. However, this argument is not about the state of souls after death but rather about the existence of the resurrection. Jesus emphasizes that God's power transcends time and death, making the resurrection a necessary reality.

Argument 7: Body and Soul Reunited (Ezekiel's Vision)

The account in Ezekiel 37, known as the Valley of Dry Bones, describes a vision where dry bones come together and receive flesh and breath, coming back to life. This account focuses on the physical aspect of resurrection, with no mention of souls reuniting with bodies. It illustrates that life is restored through breath, aligning with the concept of physical resurrection rather than immortal souls.

Conclusion

Through careful analysis of biblical passages, it challenges the conventional interpretations of these arguments and suggests alternative viewpoints that emphasize the importance of the resurrection as the key moment for believers to be reunited with Christ.

The exceptions of Enoch and Elijah are noted but do not necessarily apply to the general fate of all individuals after death, as these cases involve unique circumstances where these individuals did not experience physical death.

Questions for Reflection or Group Study Discussion

1. Did the passages and arguments presented in this chapter change your view on the topic? Why or why not?

2. What passages had you not previously considered regarding this topic?

3. If your understanding differed from what was presented in this chapter, how was it different, and how did you come to have that understanding?

4. Regardless of your final position on the topic (agree or disagree), did you learn anything new? If so, what?

PART 3
Eight Other Misconceptions

Chapter Three

The Deeper Meaning of Biblical Fasting

The Bible mentions the word *fasting* or some variation of it in approximately fifty-five verses. It is not entirely forthcoming, however, in explaining the mechanics of how it is done other than going without food. As for its purpose, there are many opinions, but a common and general understanding might go something as follows.

First and foremost, fasting means to abstain from eating food for some predefined period. This denial should bring awareness to our physical dependencies and help us redirect our focus toward that which is spiritual. Subsequently, it helps us to commune better with God, deepening our prayers and devotional time and making us more receptive to God's voice and leading. In addition to the spiritual deepening purpose, we might fast when specifically seeking God's involvement or favor in a difficult situation. It is not uncommon to hear someone say that they are fasting for the healing of a friend or loved one.

How much of this does the Bible support? Is it really about getting spiritual, about focus, about readying ourselves to hear from God? While I would agree that fasting helps with these things, scripture gives us a much different purpose for fasting than what we commonly see today.

Mourning

Of the fifty-plus verses that speak about fasting, approximately twenty-eight of them speak of fasting while in a state of mourning or fasting as a convention of mourning, where deep sorrow and grieving are found. That's roughly half of all the times that fasting is mentioned. We should let that sink in. We need to consider that there may be a disconnect in our current understanding if fasting does not somehow, in some instances, include mourning, and vice versa.

Let's begin with a couple of verses from Jesus Himself responding to a question about the practice of fasting.

> *Then the disciples of John came to him, saying, "Why do we and the Pharisees fast, but your disciples do not fast?" And Jesus said to them, "Can the wedding guests mourn as long as the bridegroom is with them? The days will come when the bridegroom is taken away from them, and then they will fast." (Matthew 9:14-15 ESV)*

Matthew quotes Jesus using the word *mourn* as a direct substitution for the word *fast*. He uses one word for the other interchangeably. This idea of fasting for the dead might be surprising to you (as it was for me) if the norm for you is to go to someone's house after a funeral to have a bite to eat.

Another account where fasting is done, maybe even expected as part of the mourning process, is found in the pages of King David's story. After David's affair with Bathsheba, the prophet Nathan rebukes David and tells him that the son born to him will die. After Nathan leaves David, the child becomes ill.

> *David therefore sought God on behalf of the child. And David fasted and went in and lay all night on the ground. (2 Samuel 12:16 ESV)*

David fasts and is inconsolable for seven days until the child dies. After the child's death, David gets up and finally decides to eat. After which we read this exchange between him and his servants.

> *Then his servants said to him, "What is this thing that you have done? You fasted and wept for the child while he was alive; but when the child died, you arose and ate food." He said, "While the child was still alive, I fasted and wept, for I said, 'Who knows whether the LORD will be gracious to me, that the child may live?' But now he is dead. Why should I fast? Can I bring him back again? I shall go to him, but he will not return to me." (2 Samuel 12:21-23 ESV)*

The servants seem to be confused, asking David why he fasted before the child died and not after. It seems that in their minds, David did something wrong. The fasting should have happened after the child's death instead of before, or perhaps in addition to. This certainly supports Jesus' idea about fasting and mourning for the dead.

David fasted for a different reason than what his servants expected. I don't want to assume too much into the text, but it appears that David was hoping that God would see his brokenness and grant him grace. Was he wrong, or were both types of fasting legitimate and David simply chose one over the other? We will come to that answer a bit below, but one thing is for sure: his servants expected fasting while in mourning.

This connection is also found in part of a story that is told in at least three books in the Old Testament. It is the telling of the people's response when the first king of Israel, Saul, is killed in battle. All three accounts (1 Samuel, 2 Samuel, 1 Chronicles) are the same.

> *And they mourned and wept and fasted until evening for Saul and for Jonathan his son and for the people of the LORD and for the house of Israel, because they had fallen by the sword. (2 Samuel 1:12 ESV)*

We see that fasting was a convention of mourning for the dead. We should also notice in this passage that mourning and fasting weren't only done for the dead but also for those who were left behind. This is an interesting twist. Yet perhaps one that will make a bit more sense as we continue to uncover the true purpose of fasting.

Mourning in its true sense of sorrow and grief is not limited to the loss of a departed one. General loss is just as likely to lead us into a state of mourning. When Nehemiah gets word of the horrible condition of Jerusalem after the Babylonian exile, stricken with sorrow, he pens this:

> *As soon as I heard these words I sat down and wept and mourned for days, and I continued fasting and praying before the God of heaven. (Nehemiah 1:4 ESV)*

It is interesting how this statement reads. Nehemiah says that he wept and mourned for days. Then he says that he *"continued fasting"* although up until this point in the text, he had not said that he had been doing so. Why use the word *continued*? Perhaps it was because fasting went without saying. If fasting was a convention of mourning, then Nehemiah would only need to say that he was mourning for the reader to understand that he was also fasting.

Sorrow of guilt

Other types of situations can cause great sorrow that don't necessarily come from loss. Let us look at other scripture where fasting is tied to the sorrow of guilt, the realization of a wrong done, a sin succumbed to, or a hurt caused to a loved one (especially God), be it on purpose or otherwise.

Time and time again, we read how God's people were confronted by the prophets and rebuked for their sins. In many of these accounts, filled with grief for what they had done, we see them respond with physical acts, one of which was fasting.

When God sent Samuel to rebuke the people of Israel for their sins, this is how they responded.

> *So they gathered at Mizpah and drew water and poured it out before the LORD and fasted on that day and said there, "We have sinned against the LORD." And Samuel judged the people of Israel at Mizpah. (1 Samuel 7:6 ESV)*

When God sent the prophet Jonah to Nineveh to warn them concerning their sin, this is how they responded.

> *And the people of Nineveh believed God. They called for a fast and put on sackcloth, from the greatest of them to the least of them. (Jonah 3:5 ESV)*

When God sent the prophet Elijah to rebuke King Ahab, this is how he responded.

> *And when Ahab heard those words, he tore his clothes and put sackcloth on his flesh and fasted and lay in sackcloth and went about dejectedly. (1 King 21:27 ESV)*

After the Jews are back from Babylonian captivity and confronted by Ezra, the priest, for their conduct and sin, this is how they repent before the Lord.

Now on the twenty-fourth day of this month the people of Israel were assembled with fasting and in sackcloth, and with earth on their heads. (Nehemiah 9:1 ESV)

As we can see, the act of fasting in these verses plays a different role from what we saw previously. Here, fasting is an expression of regret. The sorrow is not for something lost but for something done.

Purpose

We also see other expressions that are combined with fasting. We should consider the purpose of these acts — fasting, dressing in sackcloth, throwing dirt on their heads, etc. We can see that they are physical acts against one's own body — depriving it of food and subjecting it to discomfort and shame.

Nothing is worse than seeing a person who has committed a wrong going about their business as if nothing happened. Well, this is the opposite of that. Here, we get a visible representation of what is happening in a person's heart — the hurt, the sorrow, and the regret, visible to all.

The feeling of sorrow or regret did not send these people into their rooms to quietly cry and reflect on their life choices; instead, all was felt on the inside and physically expressed on the outside. This should make us question how God might feel about the phrase, "God knows my heart," when what we really mean is, "He doesn't care about my actions." More on this later.

I suspect that for some, this might be new. Fasting as a response to sorrow, guilt, or shame is not something typically seen these days. Yes, many people go without eating when they feel those things, but it's usually because they have no appetite and not something that is done as a purposeful response.

Worship

The next type of fasting moves us away from mourning, grief, and sorrow. It is not about loss or regret. The purpose of this fasting is one of worship.

Luke tells us about a prophetess named Anna who was at the temple when Mary and Joseph brought Jesus to be presented to the Lord. Anna had been married for seven years, and when her husband died, she dedicated herself to the temple. Luke tells us this.

> *and then as a widow until she was eighty-four. She did not depart from the temple, worshiping with fasting and prayer night and day. (Luke 2:37 ESV)*

We can see that although she had been a widow for many years, she was not fasting for any kind of sorrow, instead, she was doing it as an act of worship.

In the Book of Acts, we read the account of when the Holy Spirit set Paul and Barnabas aside for a special mission. Again, we see fasting mentioned alongside worship.

> *While they were worshiping the Lord and fasting, the Holy Spirit said, "Set apart for me Barnabas and Saul for the work to which I have called them."*

> *Then after fasting and praying they laid their hands on them and sent them off. (Acts 13:2-3 ESV)*

This could feel a bit perplexing. Mourning and worship are two very different things. What does fasting achieve that might be connected to these two expressions?

It seems that fasting and the other physical expressions were ways to bring one's physical body in line with what was happening on the inside. Think of the expression, "I love my children wholeheartedly, mind, body, and soul." We all understand that wholeheartedly means the whole of the person, even though the true role of the body in that statement might be a bit fuzzy since, for many, the word *love* is an internal thing.

In our society today, it seems as if people want to hide how they feel. Or perhaps better stated, how they are doing. We hide our hurt, our insecurities, and our shame. On the outside, we look fine, but on the inside, we are dying. We do it even though we all know how unhealthy it is.

That attitude is not what we find in scripture. In those days, if you were especially grateful for something God did in your life, you wouldn't quietly pray a couple of words of gratitude; you would build an altar or offer a sacrifice. And if you were grieving, you tore your clothes, threw dirt on your head, or fasted. In this way, you express yourself fully, mind, body, and soul.

Commanded by God

It is difficult to know if these physical actions were a cultural thing or part of God's original design. What we know is that God accepted these expressions, expected them, and even commanded them.

Let's look at a verse in Leviticus in three different Bible translations.

> *On exactly the tenth day of this seventh month is the day of atonement; it shall be a holy convocation for you, and you shall humble your souls and present an offering by fire to the LORD. (Leviticus 23:27 NASB)*

> *Now on the tenth day of this seventh month is the Day of Atonement. It shall be for you a time of holy convocation, and you shall afflict yourselves and present a food offering to the LORD. (Leviticus 23:27 ESV)*

> *The tenth day of this seventh month is the Day of Atonement. Hold a sacred assembly and deny yourselves, and present a food offering to the LORD. (Leviticus 23:27 NIV)*

We see here that the word *humble* is translated as *affliction* and as *denial*. This opens the door for us to examine the next reason for fasting, which is humility.

Humility

While most people know what humility is, Biblically speaking, not everyone might understand how a person would get there or perhaps show it. In scripture, we often hear God telling Israel to humble themselves or a person saying that they humbled themselves before the Lord. Is humbling oneself a simple act of reorienting how we think of ourselves? Not according to scripture. Let's look at a verse in Psalms in two different Bible translations:

> *But I, when they were sick— I wore sackcloth; I afflicted myself with fasting... (Psalm 35:13 ESV)*

> *Yet when they were ill, I put on sackcloth and humbled myself with fasting... (Psalms 35:13 NIV)*

The words *humbled* and *afflicted* are used interchangeably as we saw in the verse in Leviticus. When most of us think about humbling ourselves, we typically don't have affliction in mind. Instead, we think about examining our hearts and somehow ridding ourselves of any thoughts of grandeur, entitlement, or importance. For us today, this is a mental exercise. In Biblical times, that is not what humbling yourself looked like. The act of humbling yourself was an act of physically afflicting yourself. We already saw these expressions: the tearing of clothes, wearing sackcloth, throwing dirt on your head, and fasting. You didn't will yourself into a humble posture, you assaulted yourself into it.

King David, the author of Psalm 35, was looking for God's favor, but he knew that he needed to bring his petition to God, not as a great king of a nation but as a humble servant.

Of the many elements that make up Christianity, the one that should be floating to the top of your mind right about now is that God opposes the proud but gives grace to the humble (1 Peter 5:5).

This is key. Many people today fast when seeking God's favor but don't understand that going hungry is not the goal and that achieving a humble spirit is. Fasting is not the exchange of food for God's ear. God's not paying more attention to your prayers because you didn't eat. Coming to Him with a humbled spirit and body is what gets us His grace. If fasting does not first achieve its intended goal of humbling us, we make ourselves hungry for nothing.

Seeking God's favor

God's people of the Old Testament understood this about fasting when wanting God's favor.

> *Then I proclaimed a fast there, at the river Ahava, that we might humble ourselves before our God, to seek from him a safe journey for ourselves, our children, and all our goods...*
>
> *So we fasted and implored our God for this, and he listened to our entreaty. (Ezra 8:21, 23 ESV)*

Seeking God's protection during their travels, Ezra and the people fasted. Notice that, like David, they fasted to humble themselves so that they could then seek God's favor. Again, they didn't fast for safe travels, they fasted to humble themselves.

There is a story in the Book of Judges that, in its entirety, is quite bizarre. It begins with events that cause the whole of

Israel to go against one of the tribes, the tribe of Benjamin. On the first day of the battle, the tribe of Benjamin delivers a spectacular blow against Israel, killing 22,000 men. The next day, they destroyed 18,000. Not willing to give up because they believe their cause is a noble one, the whole of Israel turns again to God.

> *Then all the people of Israel, the whole army, went up and came to Bethel and wept. They sat there before the LORD and fasted that day until evening, and offered burnt offerings and peace offerings before the LORD. And the people of Israel inquired of the LORD (for the ark of the covenant of God was there in those days, (Judges 20:26-27 ESV)*

The sorrow in these verses seems to be double. On the one hand, they lost many of their brothers in the battle, and on the other, the fight and the threat are not over. As they look to God for comfort, courage, and direction, they lead with mourning and fasting.

In the Book of Esther, we see a similar response to a threat. The villain of the story is a man named Haman, and he has convinced the king to decree the destruction of the Jews. When word of this reached the Jews, this is how they responded:

> *And in every province, wherever the king's command and his decree reached, there was great mourning among the Jews, with fasting and weep-*

ing and lamenting, and many of them lay in sackcloth and ashes. (Esther 4:3 ESV)

When Esther is talked into going before the king to petition his mercy, she asks the people to fast for three days on her behalf. It might be easy to miss, but her petition to the people is inconspicuously missing the call to pray or cry out to God.

Go, gather all the Jews to be found in Susa, and hold a fast on my behalf, and do not eat or drink for three days, night or day. I and my young women will also fast as you do. Then I will go to the king, though it is against the law, and if I perish, I perish. (Esther 4:16 ESV)

The Jewish historian Josephus, when retelling the story of Esther, confirms that there was prayer and crying out to God. Why then is prayer not mentioned in these verses? In fact, in the whole Book of Esther, prayer is not mentioned once. Perhaps prayer is not mentioned because it is a given. Telling people to fast was the same as telling them to pray; perhaps even the more proper way to pray, which is to say, in total humility.

Did God expect this type of physical expression back then and does He expect it now? We've already started answering this question above, let's look at what the prophet Joel has to say.

Consecrate a fast; call a solemn assembly. Gather the elders and all the inhabitants of the land to the

> *house of the LORD your God, and cry out to the LORD. (Joel 1:14 ESV)*

> *"Yet even now," declares the LORD, "return to me with all your heart, with fasting, with weeping, and with mourning;" (Joel 2:12 ESV)*

> *Blow the trumpet in Zion; consecrate a fast; call a solemn assembly; (Joel 2:15 ESV)*

God Himself calls for His people to return to Him, not with repentant hearts but with fasting, weeping, and mourning. In other words, humility, which, as we saw earlier, includes the whole of the person.

It is interesting that the word *repent*, while implied, is never used here. In fact, not in the entire Book of Joel. What can we make of this? It is a common thing to think of repentance as something that happens on the inside of a person, something of the heart. But should we be considering these outward expressions that God seems to be looking for as we seek His forgiveness, His favor, and His direction? It's easy to say that God knows the heart and, therefore, we need not do more, but these verses seem to continue to challenge that mindset.

To drive the point home, notice that the act of fasting, according to God's words here, has stimulant effects on God's attention to our cries.

> *Though they fast, I will not hear their cry, and though they offer burnt offering and grain offering, I will not accept them. But I will consume*

*them by the sword, by famine, and by pestilence.
(Jeremiah 14:12 ESV)*

Although written from a negative stance, the idea is that fasting is where we start before crying out to God (which we have seen in several verses so far). And it seems to be a bit more than bringing a humble heart, for how does anyone know that they are presenting themselves as truly humble? The act of fasting, the afflicting of the body, seems to be what brings truth to stating our humbleness, the proof of a body and soul that's been made humble by being afflicted into that position.

As I write these words, I can't help wondering if when we cry out to God, "Lord, are you listening?" God is saying back, "How can I, I don't see you fasting?" We see this idea in the Book of Isaiah, where the people expect God to respond to them because they have fasted and "humbled" themselves.

Why have we fasted, and you see it not? Why have we humbled ourselves, and you take no knowledge of it? . . . (Isaiah 58:3 ESV)

In this verse, God is mimicking what the people are thinking. Complaining because God is not responding to their petitions. They are saying, "You are not hearing our cries even though we humbled ourselves with fasting," understanding that fasting was a prerequisite for God hearing their cries. But it's more than just going without food. Let's look at the rest of the verse and the next.

> *... Behold, in the day of your fast you seek your own pleasure, and oppress all your workers. Behold, you fast only to quarrel and to fight and to hit with a wicked fist. Fasting like yours this day will not make your voice to be heard on high. (Isaiah 58:3-4 ESV)*

It seems that if we want our cries to be heard, our fasting cannot be tainted. Not with selfish ambition, injustice, or conflict with others. We see a similar rebuke from God when a delegate from Bethel asks if they should continue to fast on the anniversary of the fall of Jerusalem as they had done for so many years.

> *Say to all the people of the land and the priests, 'When you fasted and mourned in the fifth month and in the seventh, for these seventy years, was it for me that you fasted? And when you were eating and drinking, were you not just feasting for yourselves? (Zechariah 7:5-6 ESV)*

> *This is what the LORD Almighty said: 'Administer true justice; show mercy and compassion to one another (v9)*

God's questions here are interesting. He asks if when they fasted, they did it for Him. That gives us a slightly different perspective to consider. The sense seems to be that they didn't have God in mind when they fasted or even when they celebrated the feasts. This might be troublesome for those of us who, up until now, have used fasting to get something from God without considering that the fasting was supposed to be done for God, not for the thing itself.

Additionally, true humility must be achieved. Both in the physical expression and in the heart. Jesus affirms this in His parable of the Pharisee and the Tax Collector.

> *"Two men went up to the temple to pray, one a Pharisee and the other a tax collector. The Pharisee stood by himself and prayed: 'God, I thank you that I am not like other people—robbers, evildoers, adulterers—or even like this tax collector. I fast twice a week and give a tenth of all I get.' "But the tax collector stood at a distance. He would not even look up to heaven, but beat his breast and said, 'God, have mercy on me, a sinner.' "I tell you that this man, rather than the other, went home justified before God. For all those who exalt themselves will be humbled, and those who humble themselves will be exalted." (Luke 18:10-14 NIV)*

The Pharisee, although dedicated to his religious rite (fasting), counted it as an act of piety instead of allowing the expression to accomplish what it was meant to do. In other words, he did the right thing for the wrong reason. Thereby nullifying whatever effect fasting was supposed to birth. This poor Pharisee went home unjustified.

Jesus warns us of falling into this trap when He touches on the subject of hypocrisy.

> *And when you fast, do not look gloomy like the hypocrites, for they disfigure their faces that their fasting may be seen by others. Truly, I say to you, they have received their reward. (Matthew 6:16 ESV)*

In other words, announcing to the world that we are fasting is considered boasting, which has the opposite effect of what fasting is intended to do.

And so, we have seen a different fasting in scripture than the one that is most often done by the body of believers today. In the Bible, we see fasting when in a state of grieving, as an act of worship, and to achieve a state of humbleness, so that we may approach God with our petitions. In today's culture, many of us have never heard of the first two reasons for fasting, and we typically only think of fasting when we are looking to bring our petitions before the Lord and want His favor. But even then, we skip the whole humility thing because most of us have never been taught the true purpose of fasting, as seen in scripture.

If we are to only cling to the third type of fasting, perhaps we should at least consider teaching it to others correctly. If someone tells you that they are going through a tough time and they ask how they should bring their problems to God, tell them to humble themselves. If they ask how that is done, tell them to consider affliction. If they ask how to do that, then tell them to fast. At least, in this way, they won't be going hungry for nothing.

SUMMARY

This chapter explores the concept of fasting, as mentioned in the Bible, and sheds light on its various purposes. The chapter highlights that fasting is not just about abstaining from food but serves different functions in scripture. It emphasizes that fasting is often connected to mourning, grief, and sorrow and that it was commonly practiced as an expression of profound sadness. Several biblical passages are cited to support this perspective, including instances where fasting is tied to mourning for the dead, seeking God's favor in difficult situations, or expressing regret for wrongdoing.

The chapter also discusses fasting as an act of worship, citing examples of individuals who fasted as part of their devotion to God. Furthermore, the chapter emphasizes the role of fasting in achieving humility before God, pointing out that it involves physical acts of affliction and self-denial to align the body with the inner disposition of the heart. The chapter underscores the importance of fasting as a means of humbling oneself before God rather than simply a method for seeking His favor.

Questions for Reflection or Group Study Discussion

1. Did the passages and arguments presented in this chapter change your view on the topic? Why or why not?

2. What passages had you not previously considered regarding this topic?

3. If your understanding differed from what was presented in this chapter, how was it different, and how did you come to have that understanding?

4. Regardless of your final position on the topic (agree or disagree), did you learn anything new? If so, what?

Chapter Four

The Many Facets of Baptism

A cursory search on the topic of baptism will yield varied definitions, thoughts, and ideas. Some say that it is needed for salvation, while others say that it is simply an expression of faith that does not affect salvation in the least. Some say that baptism predates the Bible and that it was taken from other cultures and religions. Some compare Old Testament ritual washings to New Testament baptism and say that it is the same thing or at least very similar. And some even say that it washes away the original sin of Adam and Eve. So, what does the Bible say?

In this chapter, we will cover all things having to do with baptism, including Holy Spirit baptism. The only real exception will be regarding the question of why Jesus got baptized, which is covered in another chapter.

Other religions

First, let's get the idea of baptism predating the Bible or being founded by other religions out of the way. The idea behind this is of no consequence whatsoever because all things were created by God anyway. Anything that man has been able to conceive has been created by or allowed by God. Whether God invented baptism before writing the Bible, during, or after, makes no difference. Wherever the idea was birthed, it was not outside of God's allowance. And when He decided to use it in the Bible, it wasn't because He thought that someone had a good idea and He was going to borrow it.

Baptism is a Christian thing

The Christian's focus should be on the meaning and significance of that thing called baptism that Jesus commands His followers to do. If you've been a Christian for more than five minutes and haven't yet gotten baptized, stop reading right now and go get baptized. Why? Because Jesus said so. No one needs me or anyone else giving them a "better" reason beyond that.

Having said that, I do believe there is value in knowing its significance — if for no other reason than to be accurate when speaking to someone who is not yet a Christian. Additionally, understanding it more fully might make it more meaningful for you as well.

The baptism that Christians recognize and embrace today is not an Old Testament thing. In fact, the word *baptism* is found nowhere in the Old Testament. That alone should alert us to consider that whatever act we see in the Old Testament that looks like baptism might be different than the baptism of the New Testament.

Ritual washings

The Old Testament has much to say about ritual washings, which is what some say is similar to the water baptism that we see in the New Testament. Most of the explanations that I have read for this comparison seem to have the purpose of proving that New Testament baptism was not a new idea and that it always existed as if that would give it more weight and make it more believable or important — in my opinion, it wouldn't, and it doesn't.

Old Testament ritual washings had a much different purpose than New Testament water baptism. Old Testament ritual washing was for purification from impurity or uncleanliness as defined by God. Such things as coming in contact with a dead body or with someone else who did, discharging certain bodily fluids, and giving birth to a child all made a person ceremonially unclean.

Here is one example verse:

> *Anyone whom the one with the discharge touches without having rinsed his hands in water shall wash his clothes and bathe himself in water and be unclean until the evening. (Leviticus 15:11 ESV)*

The focus of ritual washing was to get "ceremonially clean," which required a combination of washing and time. In some cases, other actions also included bringing a sacrifice to the priest.

Being unclean wasn't a sin, but coming before God unclean was forbidden. Therefore, God gave instructions for getting "clean" before coming into His presence. If you know even a little bit about New Testament water baptism, you can already see how it is different.

New Testament Baptism

This brings us to the baptism of the New Testament, the one which started with a man called John the Baptist. The prophet Isaiah prophesied that one day God would send a Messiah to redeem His people. The Messiah would have a forerunner — a man who would show up before Christ and announce His coming. That man was John the Baptist.

> *In those days John the Baptist came preaching in the wilderness of Judea, "Repent, for the kingdom of heaven is at hand." For this is he who was spoken of by the prophet Isaiah when he said, "The voice of one crying in the wilderness: 'Prepare the way of the Lord; make his paths straight.'" (Matthew 3:1-3 ESV)*

John was considered a prophet and a Rabbi. He offered baptism for the repentance of sins which was something not seen in the Old Testament. How John first introduced this baptism is not known. We only know that it was something that God instructed him to do. By the time we hear about it in the gospels, the Jews are already submitting to John's baptism.

> *Now John wore a garment of camel's hair and a leather belt around his waist, and his food was locusts and wild honey. Then Jerusalem and all Judea and all the region about the Jordan were going out to him, and they were baptized by him in the river Jordan, confessing their sins. (Matthew 3:4-6 ESV)*

John's fame and influence were so great that even those from the more popular religious sects came out to John.

> *But when he saw many of the Pharisees and Sadducees coming to his baptism, he said to them, "You brood of vipers! Who warned you to flee from the wrath to come? "I baptize you with water for repentance, but he who is coming after me is mightier than I, whose sandals I am not worthy to carry. He will baptize you with the Holy Spirit and fire. His winnowing fork is in his hand, and he will clear his threshing floor and gather his wheat into the barn, but the chaff he will burn with unquenchable fire." (Matthew 3:10-12 ESV)*

Three baptisms

In this passage, we see three things a person can be baptized with: water, the Holy Spirit, and fire. Some believe that fire is not to be considered a separate baptism. They believe "fire" is to be combined with "Holy Spirit," claiming that the fire simply represents purification, as in the process of purifying gold in fire. Does the Bible support this?

Let's consider John's words carefully. He begins his discourse by calling his audience (or at least some of them) a brood of vipers and asking who warned them to escape God's wrath. These are not "good" people in John's eyes. Then he says that although he baptizes with water, there is another who will "*baptize* YOU *with the Holy Spirit and fire.*" Who is the *you* that John is speaking about? It's the people listening, including the brood of vipers. Why would John use insulting words to address them and then tell them that the Messiah is going to treat them wonderfully through a great act of baptism? He wouldn't.

John is saying that while he baptizes with water, Jesus came to baptize ("all people" is inferred), some with the Holy Spirit, and others with fire. This is evident in verse twelve, where he describes what Christ is going to do, which is in two parts. One will be to gather His followers into the barn, and the other will be to cast off the unbelievers into unquenchable fire. It is clear that John is speaking of two different acts that are opposite of each other, thereby supporting the two opposing baptisms, one of Spirit and one of fire, mentioned in verse eleven. If John means to say that the Holy Spirit baptism and the fire baptism are both positive things that belong together, then why follow that statement of good news with a terrifying visual of being burned in unquenchable fire? Not to mention that verses eleven and twelve both make use of the word *fire*, and why would *fire* mean one thing in one sentence and something different in the immediately following sentence? It's not likely that it would be different. If fire is something bad in one sentence, it most likely means something bad in the next.

Customarily, when we read this passage, we tend to focus on just the part that says that Jesus will baptize with the Holy Spirit. Perhaps because we've been conditioned to ignore the fire part, assuming that it is part of the Holy Spirit baptism. This leads us to see the good news only. But that was not John's main message. This should be obvious by simply considering how John begins his discourse, calling his audience a brood of vipers. That is not how one starts a conversation if the point you want to make is that everything is going to be okay for everyone.

The main point that John was making was that the people were a mess, and he intended to warn them of judgment. To see this more clearly, we need to look at Luke's account of this same encounter, where John goes on to say a bit more than just calling them a brood of vipers. John does not focus on the Holy Spirit and the good news; his words are admonishing and threatening.

> *Bear fruits in keeping with repentance. And do not begin to say to yourselves, 'We have Abraham as our father.' For I tell you, God is able from these stones to raise up children for Abraham. Even now the axe is laid to the root of the trees. Every tree therefore that does not bear good fruit is cut down and thrown into the fire."* (Luke 3:8-9 ESV)

More evidence of this is seen in how the people respond to John's words. They get the "fire" message and want to steer clear of that judgment so they begin to ask John what they must do to avoid such a fate.

> *Tax collectors also came to be baptized and said to him, "Teacher, what shall we do?" (Luke 3:12 ESV)*

> *Soldiers also asked him, "And we, what shall we do?" And he said to them, "Do not extort money from anyone by threats or by false accusation, and be content with your wages." (Luke 3:15 ESV)*

Those who came with repentant hearts heard the good news in John's words (Holy Spirit), but they also understood that they were being called out with condemnation, judgment, and the threat of fire.

Finally, we'll look at one more verse to support this thinking. For this, we turn to Jesus.

> *for John baptized with water, but you will be baptized with the Holy Spirit not many days from now." (Acts 1:5 ESV)*

Notice that Jesus, speaking to His disciples, does not tell them that they will be baptized with fire. They're only getting baptized with the Holy Spirit since the baptism of fire is for non-believers.

Does the Bible speak about fire in some way for believers? Absolutely. It mentions fire as a way of cleansing or purifying. And in the Book of Zechariah, God tells us that He will refine

His people with fire. But this is not what John is referring to when he speaks of Jesus baptizing with fire. To assume that, we would have to do quite a bit of massaging of the text to explain the whole of John's words in this encounter.

Why are you baptizing?

The next point that we need to examine, which is sometimes taught without Biblical evidence, is related to John's encounter with the religious leaders when Pharisees sent priests and Levites to question him regarding his baptizing.

> *They asked him, "Then why are you baptizing, if you are neither the Christ, nor Elijah, nor the Prophet?" (John 1:25 ESV)*

Some say that proselyte baptism, which was done when receiving a gentile into Judaism, was prevalent during the first century. Some assert that John was being questioned here because he was treating Jews like proselytes and submitting them to a rite which implied that they were impure. But that view is problematic given the text that we have since there is no evidence in the account. It seems purely speculative.

Not only is there no evidence in the text, but there is also no evidence that proselyte baptisms were happening during John's time. The writings that we have in the Talmud point to the practice being done much later, and there is no mention of this rite in any of Josephus' (Jewish Historian) works.

Consider also that they don't ask why John is baptizing Jews; they ask why he is baptizing if he is not one of the three persons mentioned. Let's take a close look at the exchange that leads to the question.

> *And this is the testimony of John, when the Jews sent priests and Levites from Jerusalem to ask him, "Who are you?" He confessed, and did not deny, but confessed, "I am not the Christ." And they asked him, "What then? Are you Elijah?" He said, "I am not." "Are you the Prophet?" And he answered, "No." So they said to him, "Who are you? We need to give an answer to those who sent us. What do you say about yourself?" He said, "I am the voice of one crying out in the wilderness, 'Make straight the way of the Lord,' as the prophet Isaiah said." (John 1:19-23 ESV)*

So, who are these that are mentioned here, and what is their significance? Let's first consider the Prophet. Moses is told by God that He will raise up a prophet like Moses to speak to the people on God's behalf.

> *The LORD your God will raise up for you a prophet like me from among you, from your brothers—it is to him you shall listen— (Deuteronomy 18:15 ESV)*

Next, Elijah was the prophet who was taken up to heaven without actually dying. Then, in the Book of Malachi, we read this prophecy.

> *Behold, I will send you Elijah the prophet before the great and awesome day of the LORD comes. (Malachi 4:5 ESV)*

And, of course, there is the Christ, the Messiah, which we know as promised by God through all of the Old Testament.

Understanding who the Prophet, Elijah, and the Christ were to the Jews helps us understand the question. These three mentioned are tied to prophetic text. It is not the baptism of Jews that the leaders are questioning. It is prophecy that they have in mind. This question is about John's authority in the context of those prophecies, not about baptizing Jews.

If the leaders have prophecy in mind, as we just identified, then it is fitting to look to Old Testament prophecy concerning anything that might look like New Testament baptism to see if we can find the connection.

> *Wash me thoroughly from my iniquity, and cleanse me from my sin! (Psalm 51:2 ESV)*

> *I will cleanse them from all the guilt of their sin against me, and I will forgive all the guilt of their sin and rebellion against me. (Jeremiah 33:8 ESV)*

> *For I will take you out of the nations; I will gather you from all the countries and bring you back into your own land. I will sprinkle clean water on you, and you will be clean; I will cleanse you from all your impurities and from all your idols. I will give you a new heart and put a new spirit in you; I will remove from you your heart of stone and give you*

a heart of flesh. And I will put my Spirit in you and move you to follow my decrees and be careful to keep my laws. (Ezekiel 36:24-27 ESV)

It might not be obvious at first because these passages look a lot like ritual cleansing, which we've already stated are not like New Testament baptism. However, all three of these passages, two of which are prophetic, have something in common that is very important and very different from ritual cleansing. Notice who is doing the cleansing; it's God. This is different from the water cleansing the Jews were used to doing, which put the burden of washing on the person needing to be cleansed. God's command was for people to bathe themselves to get ceremonially clean. People didn't enlist others to help cleanse them — they bathed themselves. But in these passages, God is the One doing the cleansing. Note also that this cleansing is not for ceremonial uncleanliness; it is for sin.

We can see then why the leaders want to know who John is and why he is baptizing since, in their minds, that job belongs to God — or someone sent by God who might be the fulfillment of prophecy.

Preparing the way

John denies that he is any of those mentioned, although he is one that has been prophesied about — the one who would prepare the way for the Messiah.

We'll take a little detour from our current topic to look at the last verse in our text because it is another verse that is sometimes misunderstood. Let us look at the prophecy in Isaiah that was mentioned above, which John quotes.

> *A voice cries: "In the wilderness prepare the way of the LORD; make straight in the desert a highway for our God. (Isaiah 40:3 ESV)*

Notice that it reads a bit differently than how it's seen in the gospels. All four of the gospels say, "The voice of one crying in the wilderness," but Isaiah doesn't say it that way. It is infinitely more powerful the way it is worded in Isaiah. What Isaiah says is, "Prepare the way *in* the wilderness, and *in* the desert, make a straight highway for the Lord." In the wilderness, if you don't know your way around, you can easily get lost — and the wilderness is not a place where you want to get lost. In the desert, it is said that one can walk around in circles and never find their way through due to limited reference points. These are places of confusion and potential danger. Why is this significant? Because of the way this prophecy reads in the gospels, it sounds like someone is in the wilderness calling out to those who are not. But how it's worded in Isaiah, we get the sense that all peoples are in the wilderness/desert, and someone is clearing the way (in those places) to make a path for God to reach His people.

Now, back to our topic.

John's baptism, null and void

John is baptizing for the forgiveness of sins. But since Jesus takes away the sins of the world, John's baptism will no longer be needed, and John must have known it. Let us look at this statement from John.

> *The next day he saw Jesus coming toward him, and said, "Behold, the Lamb of God, who takes away the sin of the world! (John 1:29 ESV)*

We cannot miss the implication of this statement, and we wonder if even John knew the weight of it. Not only would John's baptism change or become void, but by referring to Jesus as the Lamb of God, John is letting us know that it would not be through water baptism that Jesus will perform this act, but by a personal sacrifice.

Let us look at another account where we can see how John's water baptism for the forgiveness of sins is no longer regarded as necessary. The account takes place in the Book of Acts. The Apostle Paul, while traveling through Ephesus, encounters some disciples. Paul finds out that they had been baptized by John, and so says this:

> *And Paul said, "John baptized with the baptism of repentance, telling the people to believe in the one who was to come after him, that is, Jesus." On hearing this, they were baptized in the name of the Lord Jesus. (Acts 19:4-5 ESV)*

It seems that Paul was telling them that John's baptism was not the be-all and end-all, which is why John pointed people to Jesus. And now that Jesus was on the scene, baptism was to mean something different. It is the same message that he delivered in the synagogue at Antioch in Pisidia:

> *Before his coming, John had proclaimed a baptism of repentance to all the people of Israel. (Acts 13:24 ESV)*

> *Let it be known to you therefore, brothers, that through this man forgiveness of sins is proclaimed to you, (Acts 13:38 ESV)*

In other words, John baptized for the forgiveness of sins *before* Jesus showed up, but now that Jesus has arrived, the forgiveness of sins is available through Him.

The purpose of the Christian baptism

Scripture does not give us an explicit reason why a Christian is to get baptized. It doesn't say do this because of that. It is only clear that the moment a person puts their faith in Jesus, they are to get baptized. That doesn't mean we have no information that allows us to infer the why.

The idea of an unbaptized Christian is unheard of in scripture. If you were not baptized, you were not a follower of Jesus. However, today, this is not what we see in professing Christians, with baptism being done as a separate act, sometimes years after proclaiming Jesus. In the first century, this was not the case — the minute a person accepted Christ, they were looking for water to get baptized since baptism was the ceremonial act by which a person accepted Jesus.

> *And as they were going along the road they came to some water, and the eunuch said, "See, here is water! What prevents me from being baptized?"*

(Acts 8:36 ESV)

Crispus, the ruler of the synagogue, believed in the Lord, together with his entire household. And many of the Corinthians hearing Paul believed and were baptized. (Acts 18:8 ESV)

So those who received his word were baptized, and there were added that day about three thousand souls. (Acts 2:41 ESV)

But when they believed Philip as he preached good news about the kingdom of God and the name of Jesus Christ, they were baptized, both men and women. (Acts 8:12 ESV)

Looking at all of the 80+ verses that mention baptism, many of which we are looking at here in this chapter, we see that baptism is a rite that marks our faith. It can be likened to a wedding where a couple is legally married when the necessary papers are finalized with the courts, not when the ceremony occurs. It is not the wedding ceremony that is needed for the marriage to be valid, and one is not more so married by having the ceremony. The ceremony simply marks and celebrates the act.

The apostle Paul puts it differently and gives it much more spiritual meaning. He likens baptism to a death reenactment, where we are the ones who die, and that death binds us to Jesus.

> *Do you not know that all of us who have been baptized into Christ Jesus were baptized into his death? We were buried therefore with him by baptism into death, in order that, just as Christ was raised from the dead by the glory of the Father, we too might walk in newness of life. (Romans 6:3-4 ESV)*

Immersion or sprinkle?

The actual definition of the word *baptism* is to immerse. To dye a piece of cloth, one would immerse it in the dye, and it would be brought back up a different color — that would be baptizing the cloth. Considering the verse we just read, we can see that sprinkling would not make sense as the correct method of baptism. Only full immersion paints the correct picture of being baptized into Jesus' death.

Is baptism needed for salvation?

The actual act of baptism, being dunked in the water, does not save you.

> *For by grace you have been saved through faith. And this is not your own doing; it is the gift of God, not a result of works, so that no one may boast (Ephesians 2:8-9 ESV)*

This verse is the foundation of the Christian faith. Salvation is a gift from God, and there is no work, no doing, and no act that a person can initiate to merit that gift, including baptism. By faith, we receive the gift when, by faith, we believe that Jesus is who scripture tells us He is.

However, let's also look at this from another viewpoint. The Bible mentions people who will not inherit the kingdom of God and who choose to live in unrepentant sin . . . idolaters, adulterers, the sexually immoral, etc.

It's one thing to fall short once in a while and then turn to God with a repentant heart; it's another to continue sinning unrepentantly, knowing that you are breaking God's commands and being unfaithful, acting like one who is unsaved.

So, if you know that Jesus has commanded you to get baptized, but you don't do it, then you are being disobedient. Every day that you don't get baptized is another day that you are ignoring Jesus' command and undermining Him. Unless you are on your knees repenting every night for being disobedient, then you are in the same camp as the idolater, adulterer, and sexually immoral (acting like one who is not saved). In this context, getting baptized right away takes on a new purpose.

You might still be tempted to ask that if baptism is symbolic and perhaps not needed for salvation, and God knows that I am committed to Christ, does it matter if I get baptized or not? The answer to that comes in the way of another question . . . how can you say that you are committed to Christ and not do what He commanded?

Jesus asks you this:

Why do you call me 'Lord, Lord,' and not do what I tell you? (Luke 6:46 ESV)

And also says this:

> *If you love me, you will keep my commandments. (John 14:15 ESV)*

And John says this:

> *And by this we know that we have come to know him, if we keep his commandments. Whoever says "I know him" but does not keep his commandments is a liar, and the truth is not in him, (1 John 2:3-4 ESV)*

Holy Spirit baptism

Remember that we said that Holy Spirit baptism is for the believer, while fire baptism is for the unbeliever. Let's focus on Holy Spirit baptism, what it is, how it happens, and when it happens.

The first question we can tackle is whether Holy Spirit baptism and water baptism are the same thing. The answer is no. This is what getting baptized with the Holy Spirit looks like.

> *When the day of Pentecost arrived, they were all together in one place. And suddenly there came from heaven a sound like a mighty rushing wind, and it filled the entire house where they were sitting. And divided tongues as of fire appeared to them and rested on each one of them. And they*

> *were all filled with the Holy Spirit and began to speak in other tongues as the Spirit gave them utterance. (Acts 2:1-4 ESV)*

This is what happened to the disciples after Jesus' resurrection and ascension to heaven. Jesus had promised them that they would be baptized with the Holy Spirit (Acts 1:5), and this was it.

The follow-up question that should come to mind is if being filled with the Holy Spirit, as we see here, is the same as being baptized with the Holy Spirit. In other words, is this event a baptism, or is it something else?

For this answer, we move to an account, some nine chapters later, where Peter gets called to the home of a Roman Centurion named Cornelius. As Peter is sharing the good news of Jesus with Cornelius and his household, the Holy Spirit comes upon them. Later, while Peter is retelling the story to the other apostles, this is how he recounts the moment.

> *As I began to speak, the Holy Spirit fell on them just as on us at the beginning. And I remembered the word of the Lord, how he said, 'John baptized with water, but you will be baptized with the Holy Spirit.' (Acts 11:15-16 ESV)*

Notice that Peter equates what happened to Cornelius and his household to the same thing that happened to him and the other apostles on the day of Pentecost. He also makes the connection that this is what Jesus referred to as being baptized with the Holy Spirit.

So then, how do we know that this is not equivalent to water baptism, or that it replaces it, or is a stand-in for it? For that answer, we continue reading the account of Cornelius. When Peter sees that the Holy Spirit was given to him and his household, this is how he responds.

> *"Can anyone withhold water for baptizing these people, who have received the Holy Spirit just as we have?" And he commanded them to be baptized in the name of Jesus Christ. Then they asked him to remain for some days. (Acts 10:47-48 ESV)*

In Peter's mind, water baptism and Holy Spirit baptism are two separate things, and one does not preclude the other.

We are not to look at Holy Spirit baptism the same way we look at water baptism. Water baptism is something we do; Holy Spirit baptism is something that happens to us.

Does water baptism come with the Holy Spirit?

We just saw that in the case of Cornelius, he and his household received the Holy Spirit while listening to Peter share about Jesus. In this account, then, being baptized with the Holy Spirit was not associated with water baptism, and it happened before being water baptized.

In another account, we follow Philip, who is in Samaria, spreading the good news and baptizing all who believed.

> *But when they believed Philip as he preached good news about the kingdom of God and the name*

> *of Jesus Christ, they were baptized, both men and women. (Acts 8:12 ESV)*

> *Now when the apostles at Jerusalem heard that Samaria had received the word of God, they sent to them Peter and John, who came down and prayed for them that they might receive the Holy Spirit, for he had not yet fallen on any of them, but they had only been baptized in the name of the Lord Jesus. Then they laid their hands on them, and they received the Holy Spirit. (Acts 8:14-17 ESV)*

We see here that although the people got water baptized in the name of Jesus, they did not receive the Holy Spirit. In this case, the baptism of the Holy Spirit happened when Peter and John laid hands on them after they had already been water-baptized.

Let us look at another time when both baptisms intertwine. We've already read a couple of verses from this account. Let us look at the whole of it.

> *And it happened that while Apollos was at Corinth, Paul passed through the inland country and came to Ephesus. There he found some disciples. And he said to them, "Did you receive the Holy Spirit when you believed?" And they said, "No, we have not even heard that there is a Holy Spirit." And he said, "Into what then were you baptized?" They said, "Into John's baptism." And Paul said, "John baptized with the baptism of repentance, telling the people to believe in the one who*

> *was to come after him, that is, Jesus." On hearing this, they were baptized in the name of the Lord Jesus. And when Paul had laid his hands on them, the Holy Spirit came on them, and they began speaking in tongues and prophesying. (Acts 19:1-6 ESV)*

Here too, we see that not only did they not receive the Holy Spirit when they first believed, but also not when they were baptized. It is not until Paul lays hands on them that they receive the Holy Spirit, just as what happened with Peter and John in Samaria.

But those are not the only times. This is also how Paul himself received the Holy Spirit. In the account of Paul's conversion in Damascus, the Lord calls upon Ananias to go lay hands on Paul after Paul's encounter with Jesus and having been made blind.

> *And the Lord said to him, "Rise and go to the street called Straight, and at the house of Judas look for a man of Tarsus named Saul, for behold, he is praying, and he has seen in a vision a man named Ananias come in and lay his hands on him so that he might regain his sight. (Acts 9:11-12 ESV)*

> *So Ananias departed and entered the house. And laying his hands on him he said, "Brother Saul, the Lord Jesus who appeared to you on the road by which you came has sent me so that you may regain your sight and be filled with the Holy Spirit." (Acts 9:17 ESV)*

We see clearly that the job of Ananias was to lay hands on Paul to restore his sight and to call for the filling of the Holy Spirit. Although not explicitly noted, we can assume that Paul received the Holy Spirit when Ananias laid hands on him, after which we read this:

> *And immediately something like scales fell from his eyes, and he regained his sight. Then he rose and was baptized; (Acts 9:18 ESV)*

In short, we have examples of people receiving the Holy Spirit before water baptism, and after. While I suspect that a person can receive the Holy Spirit at the time of water baptism, we don't have an example of it in scripture.

Shifting our focus just a bit, you might have a question buzzing in your head like I had when I first read these accounts. Don't believers get the Holy Spirit when they first believe?

Looking at Paul's encounter with the disciples in Ephesus (Acts 19 above), we notice that Paul does not assume that the Holy Spirit is automatically received when a person first believes, and so he asks them if they have received it.

How is it that as disciples of Jesus, they know nothing about the Holy Spirit? Since this event happens in Ephesus, it could be that these disciples have been away from Jerusalem for some time. Perhaps they are part of the group that left Jerusalem when Stephen was martyred, assuming that they were actually in Jerusalem and perhaps got baptized by John the Baptist himself. We can speculate till the cows come home, but it doesn't really matter. The point is that it is not very strange that they would not know about the Holy Spirit. When we are first introduced to Apollos in the Book of Acts, he was preaching boldly and accurately about Jesus but yet had no idea that John's water baptism was replaced by water baptism in Christ Jesus.

So, it is not strange that these disciples didn't know about the Holy Spirit. What is strange is that they are believers that don't have the Holy Spirit. It is a staple belief in Christianity that a person receives the Holy Spirit the moment they believe. So, how is it that these disciples don't have the Holy Spirit? How is it that the multitude in Samaria that Philip was baptizing did not receive the Holy Spirit when they first believed, and it took Peter and John to travel from Jerusalem to lay hands on them? And how is it that the leaders in Jerusalem, Philip, Peter, John, and Paul, are not bothered by these very same questions? It seems very natural to them for a believer not to have the Holy Spirit. Although admittedly and equally unnatural to let it stay that way, which is why they go lay hands on them.

Do Christians receive the Holy Spirit when they first believe?

So far, these passages seem to contradict the idea that Christians automatically receive the Holy Spirit the moment they believe; and there is no ambiguity in the text. These passages are not interpretive; they are actual accounts depicting what did and did not happen.

Particularly in the case of Philip in Samaria, the Holy Spirit was not received when those people first believed, and as we have seen, we have other examples. Let us consider one more verse as we tackle this dilemma. In the verse below, Jesus tells us that God gives the Spirit when we ask for it.

> *If you then, though you are evil, know how to give good gifts to your children, how much more will your Father in heaven give the Holy Spirit to those who ask him!" (Luke 11:13 NIV)*

This is kind of confusing because if the Spirit is already in us, why do we need to ask for it? Does Jesus mean to say that the Holy Spirit is given in measure? If so, would it not have been more appropriate to say, "give **of** the Holy Spirit," instead of, "give **the** Holy Spirit?"

The idea that we receive the Holy Spirit the moment we believe is not explicitly found in scripture. Like the idea of the Trinity, it is found by examining the many verses that touch on the topic. The closest verse we have that seems to say that we receive the Spirit the moment we believe is found in the account where Peter gives his first sermon at Pentecost.

> *Now when they heard this they were cut to the heart, and said to Peter and the rest of the apostles, "Brothers, what shall we do?" And Peter said to them, "Repent and be baptized every one of you in the name of Jesus Christ for the forgiveness of your sins, and you will receive the gift of the Holy Spirit. (Acts 2:37-38 ESV)*

This account is more interesting than what we might first realize. Did you notice that Peter never tells them that they must believe? His response to their question regarding what they must do is to repent and be baptized, but he does not mention that they must believe. How do we process that? It seems that the reason is because they already believe. Their belief is what prompts their question. No one would have asked what they needed to do in response to what they heard if they did not believe all that Peter had just finished telling them. Knowing this, Peter jumps to the next logical thing for a believer to do: repent and be baptized. This tells us, then, that they did not receive the Spirit when they first believed. In this account, according to Peter, it will take the act of repentance and baptism for that to happen.

Where does this leave us regarding the time a believer receives the Holy Spirit? The Bible is clear that the Spirit is promised and given to those who truly believe. While many verses, especially in Paul's letters, seem to suggest that it is when we first believe, we have good Biblical evidence showing that this was not always the case. This might lead us to wonder if it is a case that might happen today. While this is a valid question, it might not be one of much concern since Jesus tells us that God gives the Holy Spirit to those who ask — so if in doubt, just ask.

SUMMARY

This chapter explores various aspects of this Christian practice of Baptism and examines its biblical origins and significance.

- The chapter begins by acknowledging the diversity of opinions on baptism, ranging from its role in salvation to its historical roots in other cultures and religions. The chapter emphasizes that regardless of its origins, baptism is a command of Jesus for His followers.

- The chapter distinguishes between Old Testament ritual washings, which focused on ceremonial cleanliness, and New Testament baptism, which is centered on repentance and faith in Jesus. John the Baptist's role as a forerunner to Christ is highlighted, with an emphasis on his baptism for repentance.

- The chapter explores the concept of three baptisms, namely water, Holy Spirit, and fire, explaining that they represent distinct acts with different implications. Water baptism and Holy Spirit baptism are for believers, and fire baptism represents judgment for unbelievers.

- The chapter also addresses the question of why John the Baptist baptized and suggests that it was related to Old Testament prophecies about preparing the way for the Messiah. The chapter dispels the notion that John's baptism was akin to proselyte baptism, emphasizing that it was more about fulfilling prophetic expectations.

- The chapter underscores the transformation in baptism from John's time, where it symbolized forgiveness of sins, to the Christian practice of baptism in the name of Jesus, which signifies faith in Christ and a newness of life.

- The discussion then turns to the mode of baptism, with the chapter asserting that immersion is the biblical method due to the literal meaning of the word *baptism*. The chapter concludes by addressing the question of whether baptism is necessary for salvation, affirming that salvation is by grace through faith but emphasizing the importance of obedience to Jesus' command to be baptized.

- The chapter also briefly touches on Holy Spirit baptism, distinguishing it from water baptism, and highlighting its significance as a distinct experience for believers.

- This chapter also explores the timing of when Christians receive the Holy Spirit in relation to water baptism. The chapter presents several biblical accounts to illustrate different scenarios:

    a. Cornelius and his household received the Holy Spirit while listening to Peter, before they were water-baptized. This suggests that receiving the Holy Spirit is not necessarily tied to water baptism.

    b. In Samaria, Philip baptized people who believed in

Jesus, but they did not receive the Holy Spirit until Peter and John laid hands on them after their water baptism. This suggests that receiving the Holy Spirit doesn't always happen when a person first believes.

c. In Ephesus, Paul encountered disciples who had not received the Holy Spirit even though they believed in Jesus and had been baptized by John the Baptist. They received the Holy Spirit when Paul laid hands on them after their water baptism. This, too, suggests that receiving the Holy Spirit doesn't always happen when a person first believes.

d. Paul himself received the Holy Spirit when Ananias laid hands on him after his encounter with Jesus on the road to Damascus. This presumably occurred before Paul's water baptism.

Conclusion

The chapter concludes by suggesting that while many verses, especially in Paul's letters, seem to indicate that the Holy Spirit is received when a person first believes, the biblical evidence also shows instances where this was not the case. There is also a reference to Luke 11:13, where Jesus states that God gives the Holy Spirit to those who ask for it, raising questions about whether the Spirit is given in measure. Therefore, the timing of receiving the Holy Spirit may vary, and the chapter advises that if in doubt, believers should simply ask God for the Holy Spirit.

Questions for Reflection or Group Study Discussion

1. Did the passages and arguments presented in this chapter change your view on the topic? Why or why not?

2. What passages had you not previously considered regarding this topic?

3. If your understanding was previously different than what was presented in this chapter, how was it different, and how did you come to have that understanding?

4. Regardless of your final position on the topic (agree or disagree), did you learn anything new? If so, what?

Chapter Five

Unearthing the Purpose of Jesus' Baptism

Since John's baptism was a baptism of repentance, and Jesus was without sin, why did He submit to John's baptism? There are several popular theories. Some say that it was an act of obedience, others that it was to serve as an example to Christians, others that it was to symbolize washing away the sins of the world, others that it symbolized His death and resurrection, and yet others that it served the purpose of ceremonial washing.

While all these ideas may make for a good sermon, the actual Biblical evidence is somewhat thin. That does not necessarily mean that they are all incorrect or without merit. We can learn a lot from examining how verses are interpreted and tied together by good teachers to bring reasonable understanding to passages that are not easily understood.

However, with this question specifically, we must wonder why there is not more consensus. The answer is not surprising.

The three synoptic gospels mention Jesus' baptism, but in their account, none tell us the explicit reason for it. This forces us to look elsewhere.

Jesus' baptism

Let's begin with the account that gives us the most information. Unfortunately, it's not much. This is the most we get from Matthew's account when John is hesitant to baptize Jesus:

> *But Jesus answered him, "Let it be so now, for thus it is fitting for us to fulfill all righteousness." Then he consented. (Matthew 3:15 ESV)*

These are the only explicit words that we have — that Jesus got baptized to fulfill all righteousness. But what does that mean?

For starters, the actual text says more than what most of us focus on. Examining the verse again, we see that there are two things to consider in this verse, not one. The first is fulfilling all righteousness, and the other is Jesus saying, "it is fitting for **us**..." That second phrase is the one that most of us pass over. Jesus makes a point to include John in the process. Whatever this thing is, it is proper for John and Him to be doing it together.

We get a clearer picture of the implication of "us" when we expand the verse like this: *"it is fitting for you and me to fulfill all righteousness."* And just like that, the verse seems to change — John is part of the equation.

Our question also now changes. Is Jesus saying that getting baptized will fulfill all righteousness, or is He saying that the act of John baptizing Him fulfills all righteousness? Or is it something else? When He says, "it is fitting," what is the "it?"

To understand what is happening here, we need to expand our analysis to include John.

Let's begin with who John was. At this point in scripture, John is God's prevalent prophet. Jesus Himself affirms it and calls him more than a prophet.

> *What then did you go out to see? A prophet? Yes, I tell you, and more than a prophet. (Matthew 11:9 ESV)*

Not only was he a prophet, but a prophet that was prophesied about. Isaiah and Malachi specifically tell us that this prophet was the messenger that God would send to prepare the way for the Messiah. We know that John the Baptist is that prophet because Jesus also affirms it.

> *This is he of whom it is written, "'Behold, I send my messenger before your face, who will prepare your way before you.' (Matthew 11:10 ESV)*

John's purpose was to make a path for the Messiah, his method was water baptism, and that baptism was for the forgiveness of sins.

Making a way

How exactly was John making a way for Jesus?

> *And Paul said, "John baptized with the baptism of repentance, telling the people to believe in the one who was to come after him, that is, Jesus." On hearing this, they were baptized in the name of the Lord Jesus. (Acts 19:4-5 ESV)*

That is just one example, but repeatedly and consistently, John points to Jesus in just about every recorded conversation we have of his. If John baptized you, you heard about Jesus. John not only spoke about Jesus, but he also created expectancy. It is difficult to imagine anyone walking away from being baptized by John, thinking that that was the end of it; they must have been expecting more to come.

John used water baptism as his method to reach people. A method that God had chosen. A method meant to reveal Jesus to Israel. John tells us this:

> *I myself did not know him, but for this purpose I came baptizing with water, that he might be revealed to Israel." (John 1:31 ESV)*

So, how does baptizing with water reveal Jesus? It doesn't. At least not the act itself.

The purpose of John's baptism was for the forgiveness of sins. Every Jew knew that sin was what separated them from

God, and John was offering forgiveness through water baptism. This was no small matter.

Imagine how amazing this must have been for the Jews. A people who only knew laws and sacrifices as the means to remain right with God. The significance of this cannot be overstated.

And yet, it is better than that. John's message does not stop at a baptism for the forgiveness of sins. It is a message that also announces that there is another who is greater and who takes away all sin.

This is the piece that we cannot miss. John's baptism was for the forgiveness of sins. The One to come would take away all sin. Whatever the connection, sin is at its core. And it means that John's baptism will have to give way to the One who is to come.

The only thing left now is to reveal who that is. Except for one little problem: John doesn't know who that person is. In the verse we just read, John says, *"I myself did not know him."*

It seems that John was going around letting people know about the One to come before he knew that Jesus was that person. And according to the second part of that sentence, baptism played a role in that reveal. This is clearer when John repeats his words and gives us more detail.

> *I myself did not know him, but he who sent me to baptize with water said to me, 'He on whom you see the Spirit descend and remain, this is he who baptizes with the Holy Spirit.' (John 1:33 ESV)*

In this verse, along with the previous one, John tells us why Jesus got baptized. Twice he admits that he did not know the identity of the One to come. Twice he tells us that God sent him (John) to baptize with water. And twice that, there would be a reveal. These three things are tied to one idea. John explains that how he came to know that Jesus was the One to come was by seeing what happened at His baptism, which is what God told him would happen. Without making it seem trivial (because it wasn't), it seems that given the text that we have, Jesus' baptism was simply God's great reveal of Jesus. I say simply only to mean that there was no other theological message for us to learn.

It almost sounds blasphemous to even say that, but there simply is no evidence that it was anything else. Let us consider also how the four gospels treat the event. Matthew, as we saw above, gives us only one somewhat vague verse. Mark gives us nothing more than to tell us that John baptized Jesus — not so much as a greeting between them.

> *In those days Jesus came from Nazareth of Galilee and was baptized by John in the Jordan. (Mark 1:9 ESV)*

Luke doesn't even tell us who baptized Jesus.

> *Now when all the people were baptized, and when Jesus also had been baptized and was praying, the heavens were opened, (Luke 3:21 ESV)*

Not only in the gospels but in all the rest of the New Testament, there is nothing concerning the reason for Jesus' baptism. In all the accounts, Jesus' baptism is used solely to point to the time when Jesus was revealed by having the Holy Spirit descend on Him.

Why was John hesitant?

Many people assume that John was hesitant to baptize Jesus because he knew that Jesus was the Messiah. According to John's testimony, however, he did not know that Jesus was the Messiah before baptizing Him.

> *Then Jesus came from Galilee to the Jordan to John, to be baptized by him. John would have prevented him, saying, "I need to be baptized by you, and do you come to me?" (Matthew 3:13-14 ESV)*

Since John has provided explicit testimony, we must consider that there may be another reason for John to hold Jesus in such high esteem which might have provoked that question. And there is.

John and Jesus were related. When Mary became pregnant with Jesus, she visited her relative, Elizabeth, who was already six months pregnant with John. This is what happened when Mary arrived.

> *In those days Mary arose and went with haste into the hill country, to a town in Judah, and she entered the house of Zechariah and greeted Elizabeth. And when Elizabeth heard the greeting of Mary, the baby leaped in her womb. And Elizabeth was filled with the Holy Spirit, and she ex-*

> claimed with a loud cry, "Blessed are you among women, and blessed is the fruit of your womb! And why is this granted to me that the mother of my Lord should come to me? For behold, when the sound of your greeting came to my ears, the baby in my womb leaped for joy. And blessed is she who believed that there would be a fulfillment of what was spoken to her from the Lord." (Luke 1:39-45 ESV)

It would be difficult to believe that John didn't know this story. He may not have known that Jesus was the Messiah, but undoubtedly, he knew there was something special about Jesus, as Elizabeth said, "*a blessed fruit, a fulfillment of what was spoken to her from the Lord.*"

Elizabeth and her husband Zechariah, John's father, knew John's calling. It is doubtful that they would have kept this moment from John. It would also be difficult to believe that Mary and Elizabeth never saw each other again after this encounter and that John had never met Jesus. It is more likely that over the years, there would have been times when they got together and got to know each other. Even if at no other time than during the Passover feast that occurred yearly, when all Jews traveled to Jerusalem.

Of special interest in this passage is how Elizabeth reacted to Mary when she came to her when they were both with child. Elizabeth says, "*Why is this granted to me that the mother of my Lord should come to me?*" Then, thirty years later, we read John's words to Jesus when He came to John to be baptized, "*I need to be baptized by you, and do you come to me?*" The similarity in their responses is truly poetic.

It makes perfect sense that John, who was filled with the Holy Spirit from birth, who was related to Jesus, who had heard the stories and had seen Jesus in His early years, would know Jesus as a fulfillment of God's word, albeit without knowing that Jesus was the Messiah. If this is true, and it's very likely to be, then it also makes perfect sense for John to yield with grace and respect when Jesus came to be baptized. Just like his mother had done towards Mary, Jesus' mother, so many years prior.

Witness and testimony

There is one more observation that is noteworthy. It exemplifies how God's infinite wisdom and perfect planning play out in unimaginable ways. By Jesus allowing John to baptize Him, He affirms who John is and his purpose. But not only Jesus. By God and the Holy Spirit appearing at that baptism, they join Jesus in bearing witness that what John has been saying is true. Who better to testify on your behalf? If there were any questions about John, three witnesses showed up, who, by doing so, testified that he indeed was God's prophet and spoke on God's behalf. At the same time, God and the Spirit join John in bearing witness that Jesus is indeed the One to come. Two testimonies, each with two or more witnesses, as per Jewish law. Only an infinitely creative God could orchestrate something that amazing.

SUMMARY

This chapter explores the question of why Jesus, who was sinless, chose to undergo John the Baptist's baptism, which was a baptism of repentance for the forgiveness of sins. Various theories about the reasons for Jesus' baptism are discussed, such as obedience, setting an example for Christians, symbolizing the cleansing of the world's sins, representing His death and resurrection, and serving a ceremonial purpose. The chapter acknowledges that while these theories may have merit, the explicit biblical evidence for them is limited. Instead, the chapter examines the context and significance of Jesus' baptism, drawing insights from the Bible.

- The synoptic gospels mention Jesus' baptism, but none provide an explicit reason for it, necessitating a more profound examination.

- Matthew's account mentions Jesus' baptism as fulfilling all righteousness, and the author highlights the phrase "fitting for us," implying a joint action with John.

- John the Baptist was God's prominent prophet, foretold in the Old Testament, sent to prepare the way for the Messiah.

- John's baptism offered forgiveness of sins and created expectancy among the Jews, as it promised someone greater who would take away all sin.

- John didn't initially know Jesus was the Messiah, but

he learned of Jesus' identity at the time of Jesus' baptism.

- The purpose of Jesus' baptism was to reveal Him as the One to come, with the Holy Spirit descending upon Him as a sign.

- The four gospels treat Jesus' baptism primarily as a moment of revelation.

- John the Baptist and Jesus were relatives, and their unique connection may explain John's hesitation when Jesus approached him for baptism.

- Elizabeth's recognition of Mary as "the mother of my Lord" and John's acknowledgment of Jesus as needing to baptize him both show a deep reverence for Jesus.

- This divine testimony upheld John's authenticity as God's prophet and confirmed Jesus' identity as the promised Messiah.

Conclusion

The chapter provides a unique perspective on the significance of Jesus' baptism, suggesting that its primary purpose was to serve as a divine revelation of Jesus as the One to come. While various theories about Jesus' baptism exist, the chapter emphasizes the role of John the Baptist as the forerunner and the baptism as a means of identifying Jesus as the Messiah.

Questions for Reflection or Group Study Discussion

1. Did the passages and arguments presented in this chapter change your view on the topic? Why or why not?

2. What passages had you not previously considered regarding this topic?

3. If your understanding was different than what was presented in this chapter, how was it different and how did you come to have that understanding?

4. Regardless of your final position on the topic (agree or disagree), did you learn anything new? If so, what?

Chapter Six

The Golden Rule as Defined by Jesus

Do to others as you would have them do to you.
(Luke 6:31 NIV)

What has come to be known as the Golden Rule, "Do unto others as you would have them do unto you," is one of those sayings that is used by many but understood by few in the context in which the words were spoken as found in the Book of Luke. It is surrounded by nine other magnificently crafted verses delivered by Jesus Himself.

At first glance, the rule seems to be clear enough: treat people the way you want to be treated. If you like being treated with respect, then treat others with respect. If you like to be forgiven, forgive. And if you like to be shown mercy, show mercy. However, this interpretation, though true at its core, falls enormously short of what Jesus was teaching.

It should go without saying that even in the secular world, this rule is not supposed to be a self-serving rule. Meaning, it should not be thought of as "treat others well so they can know how we want to be treated." Instead, it ought to be "consider how we like to be treated, that we may know how to treat others." So, the benefit is for others, not for us.

Responding to others

Treating people well is undoubtedly at the heart of this verse. In Jesus' teaching, however, *"do unto others"* is preceded by four verses that strongly focus not on how we should treat others but on how we should respond to how others treat us. For example, we find Jesus telling us that if someone slaps us on one cheek, our response should be to turn to them the other. In the next verse, we read that if anyone takes what belongs to us, our response should be not to demand it back.

> *But to you who are listening I say: Love your enemies, do good to those who hate you, bless those who curse you, pray for those who mistreat you. If someone slaps you on one cheek, turn to them the other also. If someone takes your coat, do not withhold your shirt from them. Give to everyone who asks you, and if anyone takes what belongs to you, do not demand it back. Do to others as you would have them do to you. (Luke 6:27-31 NIV)*

We scarcely think about how we respond to people as being under the purview of this rule. Probably because we mostly think of it as a one-way interaction, which is no interaction at all. The typical view is that of a deliveryman dropping off a package at someone's door and simply walking away. We deliver a good deed or gesture, and the job is done: a successful act of treating someone how we want to be treated.

Jesus' teaching, however, is not solely focused on delivering a good deed or gesture per se but also on our response when an undesirable "package" has been delivered to us.

This slight distinction between "treating" people and "responding" to people is most important because, as responders, we don't get to choose who we do unto, nor the circumstance under which we do unto them. Whoever comes at us, in whatever form, will be the recipient of our response.

The others

Additionally, those four preceding verses force us to examine and consider who the "others" are in the "do unto others" part of the rule. As it turns out, "others" include our enemies, those who hate us, and those who treat us with malice. Moreover, these are not trivial additions to the "others" but the prominent figures of Jesus' teaching. They are front and center. To emphasize this, the three verses that follow our golden rule flip the focus to those who love us and treat us well to announce that they are not the ones in question. Jesus could not be clearer about who the "others" are in this teaching.

Jesus tells us how we are to respond, and without a doubt, it seems a bit over the top. How can a person respond the way Jesus instructs to such horrific treatment? The answer to that lies in how we view the person that is doing unto us. Let's say that instead of an enemy, the other person is a family member or a friend, a person dear to us. Now, let's consider those four verses again. If we are trying to reconcile with a brother who is angry with us and he is lashing out, we are more likely to show restraint. If he slaps us on the face, we might suck up the slap because we understand his pain or just because he's family. If a sister borrows from us because she is in need, we may not bother to ask for repayment. Or if she takes our coat, we may feel compelled to give her more clothes as well. And as parents, we endure much more than this from our children. Now, when we view Jesus' instructions in this light, we realize that Jesus is telling us that we should treat our enemy as we would treat someone we love.

Let us look at the three verses that immediately follow our golden rule:

> *"If you love those who love you, what credit is that to you? Even sinners love those who love them. And if you do good to those who are good to you, what credit is that to you? Even sinners do that. And if you lend to those from whom you expect repayment, what credit is that to you? Even sinners lend to sinners, expecting to be repaid in full. (Luke 6:32-34 NIV)*

Jesus knows that everyone understands the concept of treating others in kind and, therefore, spends no time explaining that concept. This is obvious in these three verses, where He gives examples of good deeds performed by people who should not even know how to do good. He tells us that there is nothing special about doing for someone who can return the favor in kind. He challenges us to consider why anyone should expect any special credit for doing something quite ordinary and socially expected.

Who we are

The idea that we are to respond with love towards those who hate us also says something about who we are. Jesus says, "*Even sinners love those who love them.*" In other words, loving those who love us doesn't make us any better than the worst of the worst who also love those who love them. What makes us different is showing love to those who are undeserving of it.

Jesus concludes His teaching with the same words He used to kick it off, "love your enemies," and then He tells us why.

> *But love your enemies, do good to them, and lend to them without expecting to get anything back. Then your reward will be great, and you will be children of the Most High, because he is kind to the ungrateful and wicked. Be merciful, just as your Father is merciful. (Luke 6:35-36 NIV)*

Our enemies

As a side note, we should notice that nowhere in this teaching are the poor and the needy mentioned. Neither are orphans or widows or any other group. This is yet another indication that Jesus is not making a blanket statement about "doing unto" all people. This is all about our enemies.

Jesus here returns to the accounting part of the golden rule. He's already told us that doing what should be ordinary yields no credit and now takes it a step further. He tells us that to get credit for "doing unto others," the interaction must be with those who oppose us. Those are His parameters for yielding a reward. In short, loving, lending, and doing good to those who might respond in kind does not add to our heavenly account. It counts only when the act is towards our enemies.

If this sounds like a hard pill to swallow, then we've missed the perspective presented in these last verses. We tend to focus on the difficulty and what we might lose in an interaction with an enemy that we are being asked to love. But Jesus is promising a reward for that effort. A return for our actions to be granted by God. In other words, although our enemies won't pay us in kind, God will. And by the words here, it sounds more than just in kind. The text says that the reward will be great. From a purely investment standpoint, we simply can't lose.

But why

However, this is not the end of the story. If we miss this next part, we've missed it all. It's the why. Towards the beginning of this section, I said that the beneficiary of the rule is not the keeper of the rule but the recipient of it. And while usually this would be true, in this teaching, it isn't. We must consider the second part of Jesus' reason for loving our enemy, or we will walk away with the wrong conclusion. Keeping the golden rule, in this particular teaching, is neither for our sake nor for the sake of our enemy — it is for the sake of the Father.

Notice the line that says, *"And you will be children of the Most High."* How curious that it should even be in the text. It can't be that Jesus is saying that becoming God's children is contingent upon loving our enemy.

It is more likely that Jesus is teaching that acting like God is how we show that we are His children. In the same way that a parent is applauded or deplored for their child's good or bad behavior, so does the behavior of God's children communicate to others the kind of Father that He is. Being children of the Most High in this context means being the proper likeness of the Father. Be kind to the wicked because He is kind to them; be merciful because He is merciful. By being like Him, acting like Him, and responding like Him, we bring glory to His name, and His goodness is magnified so that all (including our enemies) may be drawn to Him. This is why He wants us to love our enemies.

As we let this entire reading sink in, it might be good to start with the end in mind. Which is to say, it is all for His glory. Every day and in every interaction and response, we should be forever asking, what will others say about our Father after an encounter with us today?

SUMMARY

This chapter discusses the concept of the "Golden Rule," which is to "do unto others as you would have them do unto you" (Luke 6:31, NIV), as spoken by Jesus in the Book of Luke.

1. The chapter emphasizes that the Golden Rule is often misunderstood and oversimplified. It goes beyond merely treating others as we want to be treated; it encompasses responding to how others treat us.

2. The chapter points out that this rule is not meant to be self-serving, where we treat others well so they will reciprocate. Instead, it should be about considering how we would like to be treated, so we can know how to extend kindness and love to others without expecting anything in return.

3. The text highlights that Jesus' teaching on the Golden Rule is preceded by verses that focus on how we should respond to mistreatment and challenges. For example, if someone slaps us, we should turn the other cheek, and if someone takes from us, we should not demand it back.

4. The chapter underscores that the "others" in "do unto others" include not only those who treat us well but also our enemies, those who hate us, and those who mistreat us. Jesus places particular emphasis on loving and responding with kindness to these individuals.

5. Jesus challenges the idea that loving those who love us or doing good to those who will reciprocate is a noteworthy act. He encourages us to show love to those who don't deserve it.

Conclusion

The chapter concludes by explaining that by following the Golden Rule in this way, we demonstrate that we are children of the Most High, reflecting God's character in our actions. Ultimately, our goal should be to bring glory to God through our interactions and responses with others.

The central message is that the Golden Rule is not just about how we treat people but also about how we respond to mistreatment, with a focus on loving our enemies and reflecting God's character in our actions.

Questions for Reflection or Group Study Discussion

1. Did the passages and arguments presented in this chapter change your view on the topic? Why or why not?

2. What passages had you not previously considered regarding this topic?

3. If your understanding differed from what was presented in this chapter, how was it different, and how did you come to have that understanding?

4. Regardless of your final position on the topic (agree or disagree), did you learn anything new? If so, what?

Chapter Seven

Exploring Fruit-Bearing Salvation

Every branch in Me that does not bear fruit He takes away (John 15:2 NKJV)

The idea of bearing fruit is found throughout the whole of the Bible. In the New Testament, it is one of the central themes of being a Christian. Jesus says that we know what a person is about by the fruit they bear. We are to understand that a true Christian is supposed to bear good fruit.

What if, however, as professing Christians, we don't bear good fruit? Are we still welcomed into the kingdom of God? If salvation comes solely by faith in Jesus, then it sounds like fruit is optional — great if we bear it, but not necessary for eternal life.

While the logic in that statement is sound, the statement has the wrong premise. It assumes that we first decide to become Christians and then we decide to become good fruit-bearing people (with the first decision being the one that truly counts.)

But that is not what the Bible says. The Bible does not distinguish between a Christian and someone who bears good fruit. In the Bible, they are the same.

I am the true vine

To understand how this works, we turn to John 15. It is where we get those precious words from Jesus, *"I am the true vine."* Even in the first few verses alone, tension exists. Particularly in the second verse, where those said to be "in Jesus" are taken away for not bearing fruit.

> *I am the true vine, and My Father is the vinedresser. Every branch in Me that does not bear fruit He takes away; and every branch that bears fruit He prunes, that it may bear more fruit. (John 15:1-2 ESV)*

When Jesus says, *"every branch in Me,"* he refers to Christians. Those who profess to be His followers. What makes them Christians is that they are connected to Christ.

Those who don't bear fruit are taken away. If they are taken away, then they are no longer "in Jesus," so can they still be called Christians? Let's take a deep dive.

There are at least three things here that need to be examined separately to bring clarity to the whole passage and to what Jesus was teaching.

We will begin with, "*I am the true vine.*" I heard a preacher once say that Jesus would use visuals from His surroundings to develop His teachings. The preacher said that perhaps Jesus and His disciples were passing by or through a garden where He saw a vine and used that to start this discourse. While it is possible that it happened that way, when Jesus said that He is the true vine, it is not likely that He was referring to an actual vine that was in view.

The vine (or vineyard) was a symbol often used to refer to the nation of Israel. Through the centuries, synagogues have adorned entryways with depictions of grapes and vines. According to the Jewish historian Josephus, a golden vine hung over the inner portal of the Second Temple. Even during the Second Revolt, the Jewish silver denarius bore a symbol of a cluster of grapes. In scripture, we can find many references to this metaphor. Here are a few:

> *Restore us, O God of hosts; Cause Your face to shine, And we shall be saved! You have brought a vine out of Egypt; You have cast out the nations, and planted it. (Psalm 80:7-8 NKJV)*

> *For the vineyard of the LORD of hosts is the house of Israel, And the men of Judah are His pleasant plant. He looked for justice, but behold, oppression; For righteousness, but behold, a cry for help. (Isaiah 5:7 NKJV)*

> *The LORD will enter into judgment With the elders of His people And His princes: "For you have eaten up the vineyard; The plunder of the poor is in*

> *your houses. (Isaiah 3:14 NKJV)*

> *Many rulers have destroyed My vineyard, They have trodden My portion underfoot; They have made My pleasant portion a desolate wilderness. (Jeremiah 12:10 NKJV)*

It is safe to say that when Jesus said that He was the true vine, the other comparative vine that He had in mind was the nation of Israel. Which sounds like a beautiful thing, and it is, except that in reading these few verses, we get a sense that something is not right. In the first example in Psalm 80, the psalmist is asking for God to save them from some calamity. Apparently, God has turned His face away from Israel. God is not happy. In Isaiah 5, God says that He was looking for justice but only found oppression. In Isaiah 3 and Jeremiah 12, God is scolding the leaders and elders of Israel for how they have treated the people.

Seeing this, we begin to understand why Jesus might want to proclaim Himself as the true vine. God expected His chosen people to produce good fruit, but they continued to fall short. We get a small sense of this when He says that He looked for justice but found oppression. Reading a bit more in the same chapter drives it home.

> *Now let me sing to my Well-beloved A song of my Beloved regarding His vineyard: My Well-beloved has a vineyard On a very fruitful hill. He dug it up and cleared out its stones, And planted it with the choicest vine. He built a tower in its midst, And also made a winepress in it; So*

He expected it to bring forth good grapes, But it brought forth wild grapes. (Isaiah 5:1-2 NKJV)

God's chosen people were supposed to be an example to the world; they were supposed to be representatives of the God Most High. Yet throughout history, God's expectations were barely met, just as with all humans.

When Jesus says that He is the true vine, He seems to be saying that He will be taking over the fruit-producing work. It will be Jesus who will live by all of God's commands; it will be Jesus who will represent the Father; it will be Jesus who will show true justice, and it will be Jesus who will bless all the nations.

Fruitless branches

The second part to examine is, "*Every branch in Me that does not bear fruit He takes away.*" Those who believe Christians cannot lose their salvation might find this verse difficult. If we interpret the words "*Every branch in Me*" as referring to Christians and the words "*takes away*" as losing salvation, then it sounds like Christians can lose their salvation.

To avoid this problem, some preachers teach that the term *takes away* means "lifts up." The idea is that God does not punish unfruitful Christians but that He lifts them up instead and gives them more support so that they may bear fruit. If you are wondering how someone might come to that conclusion, it comes from the Greek word for "*takes away*" in this verse, which is *airo*, which could also mean "lifts up." For example, when Jesus is in the wilderness being tempted by Satan, he says to Jesus that if He is the Son of God, He should throw Himself down and that God will command His angels and that in their hands they will bear Him up. That last part, "bear Him up," is the word *airō*.

But is "lifts up" the proper interpretation in this passage? Jumping down just a few verses gives us more insight to help us with this "lifts up" dilemma. Let us look at the following verses:

> *I am the vine; you are the branches. Whoever abides in me and I in him, he it is that bears much fruit, for apart from me you can do nothing. If anyone does not abide in me he is thrown away like a branch and withers; and the branches are gathered, thrown into the fire, and burned. (John 15:5-6 ESV)*

The first observation is that the branch cannot bear fruit unless it abides in the vine. When Jesus says, "*If anyone does not abide in me,*" by implication, He is also saying, "*if anyone does not bear fruit.*" Not because they don't want to bear fruit necessarily, but because they simply cannot do so since they do not abide in the vine. With that in mind, notice the similarity in the language between verses 2 and 6:

> *Every branch in Me that does not bear fruit He takes away (John 15:2 ESV)*

> *If anyone does not abide in me he is thrown away. (John 15:6 ESV)*

These two verses seem to be saying the same thing, albeit using different approaches. That tells us that "takes away" is the correct interpretation of *airō*. The term "lifts up" seems less likely — also because there is nothing in all the text in John 15 to support that idea.

Also, let us not ignore the verses we read in Psalm 80 just a few paragraphs ago: "*It is burned with fire, it is cut down.*" This is a common metaphor for God's judgment. A metaphor that Jesus here employs as "*They gather them and throw them into the fire, and they are burned.*"

Judgement?

It is difficult not to see that there is judgment for those who don't bear fruit. Where does this leave us, then? If Jesus is speaking about His followers (which He is) and saying that they will be taken away, cut off, and burned in the fire if they don't bear fruit, then it sounds like a Christian can lose their salvation for not bearing fruit.

Coming to that conclusion, however, is an alert that we got off the wrong exit. Especially if we are counting on bearing fruit as the means for salvation when we know that a person is saved by grace, not works.

Let's take a closer look at the text. The word *abide,* as used here, means "to remain." Jesus' overarching message is to remain. Bearing fruit is the result of remaining, and it seems to happen automatically if one abides in the vine. One can debate that the message is truly about bearing fruit, but it would seem pointless because they are equal to the same thing.

When we ask the question, "Can a Christian lose their salvation?" it usually brings with it the implication that it happens by either committing some kind of sin or by not bearing fruit (not being a "good" Christian). But since we receive salvation by faith and not by something we do or don't do, can we say that we can lose salvation by something we do or don't do?

What is happening here? Clearly, someone is being taken away and burned in the fire, and it seems that Jesus is referring to people who were connected to Him somehow and then were not. Is that what He was saying? The answer seems to be yes.

In the Old Testament, we read countless stories of the Israelites turning away from God, worshiping other gods over and over again. At Mount Sanai, they pledged to obey but eventually went astray. They did not abide (remain) in their One true God. Were they saved anyway? If we conclude that they were indeed saved because they were the chosen people, then we must ask the question, is there a special place in the kingdom of God for people who worship other gods? It doesn't seem likely.

In the Book of Romans, Paul deals with a similar situation that answers this question. As he preaches to the Gentiles, using the olive tree metaphor, he tells them that they are branches that God has grafted in as the Jews are being cut off.

> *You will say then, "Branches were broken off that I might be grafted in." Well said. Because of unbelief they were broken off, and you stand by faith. Do not be haughty, but fear. For if God did not spare the natural branches, He may not spare you either. Therefore consider the goodness and severity of God: on those who fell, severity; but toward you, goodness, if you continue in His goodness. Other-*

wise you also will be cut off. (Romans 11:19-22 NKJV)

Notice that Paul uses the word *fallen* regarding the Jews and having been broken off. In other words, they were once connected, and then they were not. He says that the reason for being broken off was unbelief, and by contrast, Paul tells the Gentiles that it is their faith that got them grafted in. To make sure they understand how this whole salvation thing works, Paul warns them not to get haughty, for they, too, could be cut off. Did you catch it? Paul is speaking of a situation where their salvation may be secure one minute and not secure the next. Yet is Paul speaking about salvation? Let us look at what he says just before the verses we just read; it seems clear that he is.

> *For I speak to you Gentiles; inasmuch as I am an apostle to the Gentiles, I magnify my ministry, if by any means I may provoke to jealousy those who are my flesh and **save** some of them. For if their being cast away is the reconciling of the world, what will their acceptance be but life from the dead? (Romans 11:13-15 NKJV)*

Also found in the New Testament, John records another instance where a group of people fell away. In that account, Jesus taught that He was the bread of life, and that whoever eats His flesh and drinks His blood lives forever. After a long discourse from Jesus in that chapter, John pens these words:

From that time many of His disciples went back and walked with Him no more. (John 6:66 NKJV)

We must ask the not-so-obvious question. Did these disciples receive salvation? Was their salvation secure because they had once believed in Jesus, even though they eventually walked away? Many stories in the Bible tell us of how people and groups turned away from God. Were they saved because they had once walked with God? Is the phrase "once saved, always saved" always true?

Abiding in Him

In John 15, Jesus tells the disciples to abide in Him six times. Apparently, He wanted to stress the importance of it. The inference is that not everyone stays the course, not everyone remains, and not everyone abides! He tells us that those people will be cast out, giving a gloomy outlook to the phrase, "once saved, always saved."

Having read all this, we come to the most important question posed here in this chapter . . . is Jesus talking about losing salvation, or is He talking about walking away from it?

Verse 2 seems to be referring to people who will receive Jesus as their savior but later walk away from Him. Hence His warning to abide (to remain). They won't bear fruit because they won't be attached to the vine, and so the Father will cast them away. We know that salvation is a gift that we either accept or reject. We tend to think that those who reject the gift of salvation do so when it is first offered to them. We never think that once someone accepts salvation and is a follower for any length of time, they would be foolish enough to give the gift back. We forget about Judas, a man who walked with Jesus for three years and then sold Him out to His enemies.

Verse 2 might also refer to people who claim to be followers but are not connected to the vine and never really were. These are people who attend church, call themselves Christians, and might even be seen doing some good deeds but don't in actuality abide in Jesus — people not bearing the fruit that God is looking for simply because they are not abiding. Ultimately resulting in their being cast out.

Every branch that bears fruit He prunes

The third item to examine is, *"Every branch that bears fruit He prunes, that it may bear more fruit."* To some people, this part of the verse might conjure up some anxiety. We just read what happens to those who don't bear fruit, which might lead us to ask if we are bearing any fruit ourselves. We might even stop to make a mental list of our latest deeds and wonder if God counts them as good or even considers them fruit at all.

Reflecting on our lives and the fruit that we might or might not be bearing is a good thing. It is one of the ways that we might assess our walk with God. And yet, it could also be bad. Why is that? Because what we consider good fruit might not be what God considers good fruit. Let us bring our attention again to a verse that we saw above:

> *He dug it up and cleared out its stones, And planted it with the choicest vine. He built a tower in its midst, And also made a winepress in it; So He expected it to bring forth good grapes, But it brought forth wild grapes. (Isaiah 5:2 NKJV)*

Notice that the vine produced fruit but not the kind that God was expecting, it was wild. In other words, not good. This particular vine, the nation of Israel, was producing the wrong kind of fruit.

Bearing good fruit

So, how do we know if we are bearing fruit, the right kind, and enough of it? And is that even the right question? Perhaps not. Examining our text again, we should notice that Jesus never asks His disciples to bear fruit. His instructions are for them to abide in Him. Bearing fruit will happen automatically, and it will be the right fruit because Jesus is the vine. And since God Himself is pruning the branches, we know the pruning will get done right, and there will be even more fruit. Our job, then, is not to worry about the fruit but to abide in Jesus, and He will take care of the fruit.

And yet, let's be clear. This doesn't mean that we sit around waiting for fruit to magically seep out of our pores. Action is still required. The act of abiding, we in Him and He in us, gives us front-row seats to who He is, what He stands for, and how He loves. And we learn to be like Him, to respond like Him, and love like Him. And by doing all things like Him, we cannot help but bear good fruit.

How, then, do we abide in Jesus? Well, what's your prayer life like? What's your Bible study life like? What's your accountability and fellowship time like? What's your church life like? These are all Jesus-centered activities that help us remain close to Him. If you want to know if you are abiding in Jesus, perhaps you may want to start by examining how much time you are spending in these areas of your life. If you add up all your Jesus-centered hours in a given week, which has 168 hours, and they equal to no more than 4 or 5, can you really say that you are abiding in Jesus?

It should not be necessary to point out that it is not just about the number of hours but more so about the heart that we bring into those hours. One that is open, in submission, and willing to bear the fruit that He, the true vine, produces; the fruit that is truly good!

SUMMARY

In this chapter, the concept of bearing fruit is explored in the context of Christian faith and salvation. The author examines Jesus' teachings in John 15, where He describes Himself as the true vine, His followers as branches, and the importance of bearing fruit. Key points from the chapter include:

- Bearing fruit is a central theme in the New Testament, and it signifies the quality of a person's Christian life.

- The chapter questions whether a lack of good fruit would impact one's salvation if salvation comes solely through faith in Jesus.

- Jesus' statement, "I am the true vine," likely draws a parallel between Himself and the nation of Israel, emphasizing the expectation of bearing good fruit.

- The passage in John 15:2, where unfruitful branches are taken away, raises questions about whether Christians can lose their salvation.

- The chapter suggests that the term "takes away" should be interpreted as a reference to judgment for someone who turns their back on the gift of salvation.

- Additional biblical passages, such as Romans 11:19-22 and John 6:66, are examined to understand situations where individuals appeared to turn away from their faith.

- The importance of abiding in Jesus is emphasized, as

abiding leads to bearing good fruit naturally.

- The chapter encourages readers to focus on abiding in Jesus through prayer, Bible study, fellowship, and church involvement to ensure they are poised to bear the right kind of fruit.

Conclusion

The chapter examines the significance of bearing fruit in the Christian faith and addresses questions related to salvation and the consequences of not bearing fruit. It highlights the importance of abiding in Jesus and maintaining a close relationship with Him to naturally produce good fruit in one's life. Ultimately, the chapter encourages readers to prioritize their connection with Jesus to ensure their faith remains vibrant and fruitful.

Questions for Reflection or Group Study Discussion

1. Did the passages and arguments presented in this chapter change your view on the topic? Why or why not?

2. What passages had you not previously considered regarding this topic?

3. If your understanding differed from what was presented in this chapter, how was it different, and how did you come to have that understanding?

4. Regardless of your final position on the topic (agree or disagree), did you learn anything new? If so, what?

Chapter Eight

Reconsidering Divine Exclusivity on Being Good

In my experience, the question of why bad things happen to good people often comes from someone who is not a Christian, asking someone who is. There are two responses that seem to be the most popular. The first is that we live in a fallen world, and therefore, we should expect bad things to happen to all people, including good ones. The other response is that the Bible says that no one is good but God alone.

This second response is interesting because it doesn't really answer the question. Instead, it renders it invalid. This means we cannot ask why bad things happen to good people because there is no such thing as a good person. But does the Bible teach that?

Good people

If no one is good but God, then what do we do with the verses in Matthew 25, where Jesus says, "*Well done, good and faithful servant*"?

Jesus also says in Luke 6:45, "*A good man out of the good treasure of his heart brings forth good; and an evil man out of the evil treasure of his heart brings forth evil.*" If there is no such thing as a good person, why would Jesus bother pointing out the contrast between a good man's treasure and that of an evil one? Wouldn't it have been more appropriate for Him to point out how a man can only do evil?

In Psalms 37:23 we read that God guides a good man through life and also delights in him, "*The steps of a good man are ordered by the LORD, And He delights in his way.*"

Proverbs 12:2 says, "*A good man obtains favor from the LORD, but a man of wicked intentions He will condemn.*" It is a verse showing the same contrast that we saw previously from Jesus. God Himself recognizes, deems to be, and applies the label good to certain persons the same way that, in contrast, He applies evil to others.

While these passages are general in nature, there are some that are person specific. This is what Luke writes of the man who asks Pilate for Jesus' body after His death on the cross:

> *Now there was a man named Joseph, from the Jewish town of Arimathea. He was a member of the council, a good and righteous man, (Luke 23:50 ESV)*

Of Paul's traveling companion, Barnabas, Luke pens this:

> *for he was a good man, full of the Holy Spirit and of faith. And a great many people were added to the Lord. (Acts 11:24 ESV)*

Those are just a few examples, but there are more; Proverbs 13:22, Ecclesiastes 2:26, Matthew 12:35, and Matthew 13:27 are all verses that speak of man being good. According to the Bible, then, there is such a thing as a good person.

Where is the evidence?

From where, then, do we get the notion that God alone is good? There are two passages that seem to be the most popular for this question. One comes from Paul, who happens to be quoting a Psalm, and the other comes from Jesus Himself. Let's first examine Paul's account.

> *What then? Are we Jews any better off? No, not at all. For we have already charged that all, both Jews and Greeks, are under sin, as it is written: "None is righteous, no, not one; no one understands; no one seeks for God. All have turned aside; together they have become worthless; no one does good, not even one." (Romans 3:9-12 ESV)*

For our reference, these are the verses that Paul is quoting:

> *To the choirmaster. Of David. The fool says in his heart, "There is no God." They are corrupt, they do abominable deeds; there is none who does good. The LORD looks down from heaven on the children of man, to see if there are any who understand, who seek after God. They have all turned aside; together they have become corrupt; there is none who does good, not even one. (Psalms 14:1-3 ESV)*

It seems straightforward; all are corrupt, and no one does good. Except that Paul, in the previous chapter, says this:

> *There will be tribulation and distress for every human being who does evil, the Jew first and also the Greek, but glory and honor and peace for everyone who does good, the Jew first and also the Greek. (Romans 2:9-10 ESV)*

Apparently, then, in Paul's mind, there are at least some people who are capable of and do good. This is not a one-off verse. Let us look at what he writes just two chapters later in the same letter:

> *For one will scarcely die for a righteous person—though perhaps for a good person one would dare even to die— (Romans 5:7 ESV)*

We notice that not only is Paul speaking about "good acts" but also "good people." Is Paul confused when he says that no one does good in Romans 3? Is he quoting Psalms without knowing what he is saying? Or is Paul simply employing a method that we all use when trying to drive a point home? I'm referring to exaggeration or, more correctly, hyperbole, just as the psalmist was doing. Just as when your friend tells you about the great party she went to and excitedly announces that *EVERYONE* was there. You understand the impossibility of the statement because you certainly were not, and neither were a million other people you could probably name.

To go around quoting Paul, who is quoting David, who was using hyperbolic language, saying that no one is good and that no one does good, is simply taking the text out of context.

Jesus said it

Let us move on to the second passage, in which we find the actual words that say that no one is good but God alone. These words are from Jesus and are recorded in the three synoptic gospels. In Mark's account, it reads like this:

> *Why do you call Me good? No one is good but One, that is, God. (Mark 10:18 ESV)*

It's tough to argue with Jesus, and we certainly are not going to, but we can't ignore all the other verses that seem to say something different. We can't act as if they don't exist. If we are going to quote Mark as a response to why bad things happen to good people, we must be ready to explain away all the other verses, some of which are from Jesus Himself. Or better yet, perhaps we should examine this account to determine the true message that Jesus means to convey.

Deciphering Jesus' teaching is not always as easy as we would want. Jesus often spoke in parables and said things that sounded like riddles, which could and did leave His audience sometimes a bit befuddled. Consider this account in Matthew:

> *While he was still speaking to the people, behold, his mother and his brothers stood outside, asking to speak to him. But he replied to the man who told him, "Who is my mother, and who are my brothers?" And stretching out his hand toward his disciples, he said, "Here are my mother and my brothers! For whoever does the will of my Father in heaven is my brother and sister and mother." (Matthew 12:46-50 ESV)*

Was Jesus denying His family? Was He saying that He no longer considered Mary His mother? Of course not. Yet that is what it sounds like. Is it possible, then, that His words in Mark are also loaded with meaning beyond the text? Let us look at that entire account to get a better picture.

> *And as he was setting out on his journey, a man ran up and knelt before him and asked him, "Good Teacher, what must I do to inherit eternal life?" And Jesus said to him, "Why do you call me good? No one is good except God alone. You know the commandments: 'Do not murder, Do not commit adultery, Do not steal, Do not bear false witness, Do not defraud, Honor your father and mother.'" (Mark 10:17-19 ESV)*

It's strange enough that Jesus would say that only God is good when in other passages He calls mere men good, and stranger still is that He also seems to deny His own goodness even though He calls Himself the Good Shepherd in John 10. Twice actually. Is He saying that He is a good shepherd but not a good teacher? There must be more to Jesus' words than meets the eye.

It's a heart thing

It is not likely that Jesus means to render those other passages void. We must consider that Jesus most often dealt with people according to what was in their inner thoughts and their hearts, so we must look for clues in the text that might shed light on what underlying issue Jesus may have been targeting.

To do that, we must consider the other gospel accounts, which give us more detail. Specifically, let us look at Matthew's account.

> *And he said to him, "Why do you ask me about what is good? There is only one who is good. If you would enter life, keep the commandments." He said to him, "Which ones?" And Jesus said, "You shall not murder, You shall not commit adultery, You shall not steal, You shall not bear false witness, Honor your father and mother, and, You shall love your neighbor as yourself." (Matthew 19:17-19 ESV)*

From his words, we can extract that this man who has come to Jesus believes that there is some deed, action, or work that he can do that might or will get him eternal life. In other words, he is relying on the law, as was every other Jew of this time. A modern-day Christian would say that there is no deed or work that can get a person eternal life and that faith in Jesus alone does that. But that would not be entirely correct. If a person could keep God's commandments perfectly and be without sin, they would be eligible for eternal life. We know this is true even from how Jesus responds when He tells this man that to have eternal life, he needs to keep the commandments instead of telling him to put his faith in Jesus.

It's about people

Jesus' exchange with the man is simply brilliant and says everything we need to know about what Jesus is targeting in the man's heart. Did you notice that when Jesus lists out the commandments, He only lists those that have to do with how we deal with other people, not God? Even when he mentions the greatest of all commandments in His list, He does not mention loving God with all his heart, soul, and mind. He only mentions loving his neighbor as himself.

This is a significant clue for us. It appears that Jesus wants the man's attention fixed on people. Just as He does with His parables, He is leading the man down a path that will allow him to come to his own conclusion and answer his own question. The exchange continues like this:

> *The young man said to him, "All these I have kept. What do I still lack?" Jesus said to him, "If you would be perfect, go, sell what you possess and give to the poor, and you will have treasure in heav-*

> *en; and come, follow me." When the young man heard this he went away sorrowful, for he had great possessions. (Matthew 19:20-22 ESV)*

We can surmise that the young man believes his performance regarding the commandments has been good — and there lies the problem. His error seems to be in estimating the degree of good needed to attain eternal life through performance. Although the Bible is not explicit in this, it seems that by telling the young man that only God is good, Jesus wants the man to consider that which is wholly good for it is only that kind of good that can fulfill the law. The kind of good in question here is the kind of good that only God is, a good that is perfect. In this context, Jesus' words, then, do not contradict the other verses that say that a man can be good since we naturally understand that it does not mean perfectly good.

At first, the young man appears to not notice Jesus' rebuke concerning what or who is good, but that changes when Jesus tells him to sell his possessions and give to the poor. As he considers these words, the young man undoubtedly realizes that his performance is not as good as he thought it was and certainly not perfect. His apprehension to sell his possessions and give to the poor proves that he did not in actuality, love his neighbor as much as himself.

It's not about Jesus

The man walks away sad, and here is where we run into another misconception in the story that is worth uncovering. We assume that the man's downtrodden disposition is due to the tough decision of having to choose between his possessions and Jesus, and unwilling to part with his possessions, he finds himself missing out on what Jesus had to offer. After all, it is perhaps what many of us have heard preached regarding this passage. While this assumption is possible, it is improbable and is in no way supported by the text.

It is likely that the man did not know that Jesus was the Messiah nor what He was effectively offering. This is a safe assumption since even the disciples were unclear about Jesus. As for the exchange, we must consider that aside from the three words from Jesus, "come follow me," the entire conversation between the man and Jesus is about the law, not about Jesus or faith. At no point does the man's focus veer away from the law, nor does Jesus try to steer him from it. The man might be considering the part about following Jesus, but his true dilemma is not choosing between his possessions and Jesus, it is about choosing between his possessions and people.

The man came to Jesus convinced that good deeds could get him eternal life. He just needed to know which deeds would do the trick. Jesus doesn't correct him in that matter, and He never reveals that He is the way to eternal life. Instead, he shows the man that he is incapable of performing those very same deeds that he is relying on, based on their criteria. The man does not walk away sad because Jesus can't help him, he goes away sad because the law can't.

SUMMARY

This chapter explores the concept of goodness in the context of Christianity and addresses the commonly held belief that "no one is good but God alone." The chapter examines various Bible verses that seem to contradict this idea by describing specific individuals as good. It also analyzes the passage in which Jesus tells a rich young man that only God is good. Key points covered in the chapter:

- Many people, particularly non-Christians, question why bad things happen to good people, prompting different responses from Christians.

- Some Christians argue that there are no truly good people, as the Bible states that "no one is good but God alone."

- The author questions whether this interpretation is accurate, as there are Bible verses that describe individuals as good, such as the "good and faithful servant" in Matthew 25.

- Other passages, including Luke 6:45 and Psalm 37:23, also suggest the existence of good people.

- The chapter examines the passage in which Jesus responds to the rich young man by saying, "No one is good except God alone," and provides a deeper analysis of the conversation.

- It suggests that Jesus uses this statement to redirect the man's focus from the law to a higher standard of goodness and perfection.

- The chapter argues that the man's sadness upon hearing Jesus's words is not about choosing between his possessions and Jesus but rather about choosing between his possessions and people.

Conclusion

The chapter challenges the common interpretation that "no one is good but God alone" by pointing out various Bible verses that describe individuals as good. It suggests that Jesus's statement to the rich young man is meant to shift the focus from law-based goodness to a higher, divine standard. The young man's sadness is not necessarily about choosing between Jesus and possessions but about realizing his inability to meet the criteria of goodness set by the law.

Questions for Reflection or Group Study Discussion

1. Did the passages and arguments presented in this chapter change your view on the topic? Why or why not?

2. What passages had you not previously considered regarding this topic?

3. If your understanding differed from what was presented in this chapter, how was it different, and how did you come to have that understanding?

4. Regardless of your final position on the topic (agree or disagree), did you learn anything new? If so, what?

Chapter Nine

Rethinking The Good Samaritan Parable

The parable of the Good Samaritan has always been one of my favorite parables. I've heard it preached and interpreted in various ways, and I must admit that I have enjoyed listening to almost all the ways it has been presented. It is the type of parable that makes a person want to cheer from a place of longing for the kindness shown by the Samaritan. What would our world look like if everyone lived ready to help as the Samaritan did even when inconvenient? And yet, have we been taught this parable as written in the pages of the Bible, or have we manipulated it to mean what we want it to mean?

An expert calls

The Biblical account begins with a man, described as an expert in the law, who brings perhaps his most pressing question to Jesus.

> *On one occasion an expert in the law stood up to test Jesus. "Teacher," he asked, "what must I do to inherit eternal life?" "What is written in the Law?" he replied. "How do you read it?" He answered, "'Love the Lord your God with all your heart and with all your soul and with all your strength and with all your mind'; and, 'Love your neighbor as yourself.'" "You have answered correctly," Jesus replied. "Do this and you will live." (Luke 10:25-28 ESV)*

One would expect Jesus to respond by talking about faith and being saved by grace, but that is not what happens. Instead, Jesus responds to the man's question with another question, one that is steeped in Old Testament thinking. As the exchange continues, Jesus finally affirms that keeping the law will get this man eternal life.

Even though it is about loving God and neighbor, it still sounds suspiciously close to merited salvation. It is verses like this one that can throw a monkey wrench into our theology. Since the Bible teaches that we are saved by grace and not by works, we are tempted to want to manipulate Jesus' words to mean something different than what they say.

A setup?

Some hold that Jesus was setting the man up for the question to follow and that He wasn't telling the man that he could obtain eternal life by keeping the law. While it is possible that Jesus was setting the man up, it's not likely that He would have lied to do so. We must remember that the Jews were still under the Mosaic law, and the New Covenant was not yet in effect since Jesus had not yet been glorified. As such, keeping the law was the appropriate response. Of course, later, the author of Hebrews expands on this idea in chapters 10 and 11, explaining that obeying God's laws was an act of faith, thereby making faith still the main ingredient of their salvation. Whether the Jews of that time saw it that way is another matter.

Justification wanted

In verse 29, we read that the man, wanting to justify himself, asks Jesus to clarify who is meant by the word *neighbor*. We get the sense that he is sure that he has kept this law in full and is confident that he knows what Jesus will say. Jesus responds with a parable.

> *Jesus replied, "A man was going down from Jerusalem to Jericho, and he fell among robbers, who stripped him and beat him and departed, leaving him half dead. Now by chance a priest was going down that road, and when he saw him he passed by on the other side. So likewise a Levite, when he came to the place and saw him, passed by on the other side. But a Samaritan, as he journeyed, came to where he was, and when he saw him, he had compassion. He went to him and bound up his wounds, pouring on oil and wine. Then he set him on his own animal and brought him to an inn and took care of him. And the next day he took out two denarii and gave them*

> *to the innkeeper, saying, 'Take care of him, and whatever more you spend, I will repay you when I come back.' Which of these three, do you think, proved to be a neighbor to the man who fell among the robbers?" He said, "The one who showed him mercy." And Jesus said to him, "You go, and do likewise." (Luke 10:30-37 ESV)*

Perhaps, like me, you have come across different thoughts about this parable, its characters, and the meaning of their actions. One of the more popular interpretations is that the Samaritan represents Jesus. A figure with ultimate compassion and the savior of all men. Another widely popular sentiment is that the expert in the law realizes that this commandment is impossible to keep, further realizing his need for a savior. However, both interpretations are unlikely.

Does the Samaritan represent Jesus?

The most common reason for misinterpretation is that we look at things out of context. But often, it is because we simply don't ask probing questions that would otherwise eliminate erroneous interpretations. For example, could the Samaritan really be a representation of Jesus? If we consider that the Samaritans and Jews were enemies, then no. The Samaritan cannot represent Jesus no matter what kind of compassionate act he may have displayed. The point of mentioning a Samaritan was to get the law expert to think about his enemy, and in this case, someone that he considered beneath him and certainly not a Jew. If Jesus meant to inject Himself in the parable as the hero, instead of using a Samaritan (an enemy and not a Jew), it is more likely that He would have used a phrase like, "a certain man", or something similar. Just as He did in every other parable. One might refer to the passages in scripture that say that we (people) are enemies of God to argue this case, and while that's the type of thinking that we ought to employ, the case falls apart because while we may be enemies of God, God is not an enemy to us, and certainly not to the Jews.

What about the part where the Samaritan takes the victim to an inn with the promise of paying for any additional expenses? That sounds suspiciously like the second coming. Perhaps you've even heard it said that the inn represents the Church that takes care of God's people until the return of Jesus, at which time they will receive their reward. If that's the case, then we should have a little chat with the innkeeper and ask him who exactly he would be expecting to come back. Would it be a Jew or a Samaritan? It is a Samaritan that the innkeeper would be expecting. If we subscribe to the notion that the Samaritan is Jesus, then the second coming is that of a Samaritan, not a Jew. This presents a theological problem.

Jesus would not likely tell a parable where He is represented as a Samaritan. Consider the story of the woman at the well and Jesus' words regarding Samaritans.

> *You worship what you do not know; we worship what we know, for salvation is from the Jews. (John 4:22 ESV)*

Would Jesus paint a picture of Himself as a person who does not know what they worship? Not likely. Not to mention the last part of that verse that says, "*for salvation is from the*

Jews", not Samaritans. The contradiction is way too great for the Samaritan to represent Jesus.

Custom-made parables

Jesus' parables are custom-made for the attending audience, and the listener is challenged to decipher which character in the parable might represent them. For example, in the parable of the prodigal son, the Pharisees and scribes listening to the account were supposed to figure out that the older son in the story represented them.

For us, reading the Bible today, we must be careful not to insert ourselves in parables that are not intended for a general audience. Instead, we should put ourselves in the shoes of the person or persons listening to the parable. Ignoring this will, more times than not, lead us to lousy interpretation. This also means we must know something about the person(s) listening.

In this case, what we know is that the man listening is most likely a Jew, and not just any Jew but one who is an expert in the Mosaic Law. We can surmise that he is also very familiar with the rest of scripture if he is an expert in the law.

With that said, let us consider what character in the parable this expert in the law might see himself as. He would not likely see himself as one of the robbers, the Samaritan, or the priest for apparent reasons. That leaves us with the Levite and the victim who had been attacked and left half-dead. Since the text tells us that he was an expert in the law, and we know that Moses charged the Levites with the administration of the law, we might be tempted to think that perhaps he relates himself to the Levite. But let's dig deeper.

We should be asking ourselves if any other information is available to us that might help us answer the question. If not in this immediate text, perhaps somewhere else. We know that Jesus often used scriptures, stories, and metaphors that His listeners were familiar with to make analogies and frame His teachings, so perhaps we should look there.

North vs South

In the second Book of Chronicles, we find a story of a conflict taking place between the southern kingdom (Judah) and the northern kingdom (Israel). From these two kingdoms came the Jews and Samaritans, respectively. In that battle, the Jews were defeated badly. The story tells us that the Samaritans, after defeating the Jews, took captive two hundred thousand Judean women, sons, and daughters. They were taken to Samaria to live as slaves. But a prophet named Oded, warned the Samaritans that it would be against God's will to carry out their plan. The Samaritans listened to the prophet and instead returned the Jews to their homeland. What is interesting are the words used to describe what the Samaritans did to return the defeated Jews home.

> *Then the men who were designated by name rose up and took the captives, and from the spoil they clothed all who were naked among them, dressed them and gave them sandals, gave them food and drink, and anointed them; and they let all the feeble ones ride on donkeys. So they brought them to their brethren at Jericho, the city of palm trees.*

> *Then they returned to Samaria. (2 Chronicles 28:15 NKJV)*

Notice the striking similarities between this account in Chronicles and Jesus' parable of the Good Samaritan.

> *Then Jesus answered and said: "A certain man went down from Jerusalem to Jericho, and fell among thieves, who stripped him of his clothing, wounded him, and departed, leaving him half dead. (Luke 10:30 NKJV)*

> *But a certain Samaritan, as he journeyed, came where he was. And when he saw him, he had compassion. So he went to him and bandaged his wounds, pouring on oil and wine; and he set him on his own animal, brought him to an inn, and took care of him. (Luke 10:33-34 NKJV)*

There are at least nine textual similarities in these two stories: badly beaten, left naked, a show of compassion, anointing with oil, dressed/bandaged, cared for, put on donkeys, Jericho as the destination, and the protagonist is a Samaritan. The law expert likely connected Jesus' parable and this event in his ancestral past. This would have put him smack in the middle of the story, not as the Levite but as the wounded man left for dead on the side of the road, just like his ancestors experienced at the hands of the Samaritans.

Love your enemy

The parable does not say if the victim was a Jew, Samaritan, or Gentile. At first glance, we might interpret the parable as saying that the Samaritan acted without prejudice since the victim's nationality is unknown. But that would not have been the case for the expert in the law. Upon hearing the parable, the man left half dead on the side of the road, as far as he was concerned, would have been a Jew. This means that his takeaway would not have been simply to love his neighbor; it would have been to love his enemy.

His realization

Earlier, we noted that some say that the law expert realizes his need for a savior because he concludes that loving his neighbor that way was impossible. But that is not likely. As noted, he had objective historical evidence of such compassion. He would have known that it really was possible to show that kind of love just as the Samaritans did with his ancestors.

Not neighbors

Something else that is usually ignored affects the teaching of this parable. We cannot miss that the priest and Levite are not considered neighbors. We should let that sink in for a bit. We tend to walk away from this parable, thinking everyone is our neighbor. While that may be true, Jesus wants to teach something beyond that.

At the end of the parable, Jesus asks the expert in the law to consider the actions of the three men who encountered the victim and decide who could be labeled a neighbor. He names, and Jesus agrees, that it's the Samaritan. Apparently, just as a tree is known by its fruit, a neighbor is known by his actions.

In this parable, Jesus points out to the law expert that a neighbor is not one who receives kindness but one who delivers it. This would be an absolute shift for the law expert and his thinking who sought a neighbor to be kind to. Notice also that he doesn't get to choose the neighbor; the neighbor chooses him.

The priest and the Levite

What about the priest and the Levite? How can we interpret their mention? For this, it is helpful to know Jesus' overarching issue with the religious leaders of their time. Two main ones are their hypocrisy and departure from the law's intent. Their hypocrisy was that they preached and commanded things that they themselves would not do, and their departure from intent was that they had elevated the law above its purpose. Rigid to perform for the sake of being counted righteous supplanted the reasons why the law existed in the first place.

When considering this, using the priest and Levite makes perfect sense. Jesus uses two examples (think two witnesses) who knew the law, perhaps better than the law expert, and either chose to ignore it blatantly (hypocrisy) or deemed that the victim did not count as a neighbor (departure from the intent of the law). And is this not the case with the law expert who wants to know who his neighbor is?

Jesus never explains why the priest and Levite don't stop to help the wounded man. Perhaps it's because a reason is unnecessary since none would be acceptable.

The neighbor within

The parable is brilliant. The law expert wants to know what he should do, but Jesus replies with what he should be. As if to say, "Don't look for the neighbor out there; look for the neighbor within."

Sometimes, we don't act because it's the right thing to do but because we can't bear the injustice. This points to law vs. love. Let us ask ourselves, what really drives and sustains our righteousness? What is more likely to move us to action, intellectually knowing it's the right thing to do or a broken heart towards the situation? I believe this is part of what Jesus was teaching. The priest and Levite knew the right thing to do, but the Samaritan was moved to action by his compassion. No wonder Jesus is so much for changing hearts instead of minds.

Even in the account of the Judean-Samaritan conflict, the Samaritans obeyed what God commanded through the prophet and did not take the Jews into captivity. They could have simply walked away from the Jews and counted it as having been obedient to God's command. Yet they did more than that. They exhibited compassion, genuinely showing love to their enemy neighbor, thereby expressing their understanding of the intent behind the law.

In the Old Testament, God commands the Jews to care for the widow, the fatherless, and the foreigner. The first two are obvious: they are vulnerable groups. But what about the foreigner? God's reason for the Jews caring for the foreigner is that they, too, were once foreigners (in Egypt). Considering the story we read in Chronicles, and knowing this command, the law expert must realize the same truth here, that he should care for his enemy because he was once the man on the side of the road who received mercy from his enemy.

SUMMARY

This chapter examines the Parable of the Good Samaritan, which is a well-known story from the Bible that illustrates the importance of compassion and loving one's neighbor.

- A law expert approaches Jesus with the question of how to inherit eternal life.

- Jesus responds with a question about the law, and the expert correctly summarizes it as loving God and neighbor.

- Jesus affirms that keeping the law leads to eternal life, which may seem contradictory to the idea of salvation by grace.

- The expert seeks to justify himself and asks who his neighbor is.

- Jesus responds with the Parable of the Good Samaritan.

- In the parable, a man is robbed and left half-dead on the road. A priest and a Levite pass by without helping, while a Samaritan shows compassion and cares for the injured man.

- The law expert is challenged to identify who acted as a neighbor in the story.

- The parable's interpretation goes beyond simply loving one's neighbor but emphasizes that a neighbor is known by their actions, not just by receiving kindness.

- The priest and Levite represent religious leaders who either ignored the law's intent or acted hypocritically.

- The parable encourages a shift from seeking a neighbor to be kind to and instead becoming a neighbor who delivers kindness.

- Jesus underscores the importance of a compassionate heart over mere intellectual understanding of what is right.

Conclusion

The Parable of the Good Samaritan challenges traditional interpretations and encourages a deeper understanding of compassion, love, and righteousness. It emphasizes that one's actions, motivated by a compassionate heart, define them as a neighbor. The parable suggests that a neighbor is not the one receiving kindness but the one delivering it. It invites reflection on whether righteousness is driven by rules and intellect or by a heartfelt sense of justice and mercy. Ultimately, the parable teaches the importance of changing hearts rather than just changing minds and highlights the transformative power of love and compassion.

Questions for Reflection or Group Study Discussion

1. Did the passages and arguments presented in this chapter change your view on the topic? Why or why not?

2. What passages had you not previously considered regarding this topic?

3. If your understanding differed from what was presented in this chapter, how was it different, and how did you come to have that understanding?

4. Regardless of your final position on the topic (agree or disagree), did you learn anything new? If so, what?

Chapter Ten

Samaria: Ancient Jewish Travel Myths

Just about every sermon that I've sat through on the topic has taught that Jews in Jesus' time avoided traveling through Samaria. It is said that due to the hatred between them and the Samaritans, they traveled around Samaria but not through it. The animosity between Jews and Samaritans is certain and depicted vividly in the Bible. The idea of avoided travel makes perfect sense, except that the Biblical evidence is sketchy at best. Let us review some of the verses that mention Samaria and see what information we can find on this opinion.

Jews and Samaritans

The reason that is used most often for the Jews hating Samaritans and not traveling through Samaria is that when the Assyrians conquered the northern kingdom of Israel, their captors brought in Gentiles to resettle the land, which resulted in something that God had been warning the nation about since forever, "Don't intermix, as it will be your demise." These three verses sum up what happened.

> *And the king of Assyria brought people from Babylon, Cuthah, Avva, Hamath, and Sephar-vaim, and placed them in the cities of Samaria instead of the people of Israel. And they took possession of Samaria and lived in its cities. (2 Kings 17:24 ESV)*

> *So these nations feared the LORD and also served their carved images. Their children did likewise, and their children's children—as their fathers did, so they do to this day. (2 Kings 17:41 ESV)*

> *For they have taken some of their daughters to be wives for themselves and for their sons, so that the holy race has mixed itself with the peoples of the lands. And in this faithlessness the hand of the officials and chief men has been foremost. (Ezra 9:2 ESV)*

So, the Samaritans were considered an impure race that worshiped other Gods besides the one true God, and for this, they were despised by the Jews. The problem, however, is that these verses and others like them are misleading if we ignore the details.

Most people simply see the city of Samaria in these verses. But look closer, and you will notice that they refer not only to the city of Samaria but to the Samaritan cities (plural). Samaria was the capital of the northern kingdom when the Assyrians invaded Israel, which at that time consisted of 10 tribes. This means that these verses don't only apply to Samaria, the capital city, but also to all the other cities in the northern kingdom. Yes, the entire northern kingdom is referred to here as Samaria.

This means that if the Jews avoided traveling through the tainted territory, the whole of the northern kingdom must be meant, not just the city of Samaria. The Britannica, like many other sources, tells us, "Following the conquest of the northern kingdom by the Assyrians in 721 BC, the ten tribes were gradually assimilated by other peoples . . ."

Jesus takes refuge in Samaria

This point is important because after Jesus brings Lazarus back from the dead, the Jewish leaders proclaim a death sentence on Jesus, which forces Him to leave and head to a town called Ephraim.

> *Jesus therefore no longer walked openly among the Jews, but went from there to the region near the wilderness, to a town called Ephraim, and there he stayed with the disciples. (John 11:54 ESV)*

It may not be apparent if your geography is rusty, but Ephraim was a northern kingdom tribe, yes, a Samaritan city. It seems odd that Jesus would find refuge in territory that supposedly was avoided at all costs. And more so that John, the author, doesn't make a big deal about it. Perhaps it was because there was no big deal to be made.

Jesus goes to Samaria

Let us continue in the Book of Luke. In this account, Jesus is headed south towards Jerusalem. In verse nine, Luke tells us that Jesus is in Bethsaida. From Matthew's and Mark's accounts, however, it appears that Jesus had moved on to His hometown of Capernaum. Between Him and Jerusalem lies the territory of Samaria.

> *When the days drew near for him to be taken up, he set his face to go to Jerusalem. And he sent messengers ahead of him, who went and entered a village of the Samaritans, to make preparations for him. But the people did not receive him, because his face was set toward Jerusalem. And when his disciples James and John saw it, they said, "Lord, do you want us to tell fire to come down from heaven and consume them?" But he turned and rebuked them. And they went on to another village.* (Luke 9:51-56 ESV)

We don't know if Jesus specifically told His messengers to go through Samaria or if it was their idea. We must assume that they at least had agreed on the village where they would meet. How else would Jesus have known where to find them? We can see that going through Samaria was a conscious thought and part of the travel plan. Noting also that if they had never been through Samaria before, how would they know which village to choose to meet at? It stands to reason that they would have been familiar with the towns of Samaria, most likely for having traveled through them in the past.

It is peculiar also that the disciples reacted so strongly when that particular village did not accommodate them. Did they not expect that kind of treatment? If, in truth, they never traveled through Samaria because of the mutual hatred, one would think that they would have been expecting the rejection.

Another thing to consider is that the messengers were not rejected, Jesus was. The messengers got there before Jesus to make preparations. We don't know how many days ahead of Jesus they were, but we can assume that the preparations were already made before Jesus reached them since it would not have made sense for them to wait for Jesus to arrive to start making preparations. There is no evidence that they had any problems until Jesus arrived. In other words, the messengers had been welcomed.

Finally, we are told that after the rejection, they simply moved on to another village. Presumably, it was a nearby village in Samaritan territory since the objective of stopping in Samaria was most likely one of rest, to stay the night before continuing to Jerusalem.

The woman at the well

The next Biblical account to consider is found in the Book of John.

> *Now when Jesus learned that the Pharisees had heard that Jesus was making and baptizing more disciples than John (although Jesus himself did not baptize, but only his disciples), he left Judea*

> *and departed again for Galilee. And he had to pass through Samaria. So he came to a town of Samaria called Sychar, near the field that Jacob had given to his son Joseph. Jacob's well was there; so Jesus, wearied as he was from his journey, was sitting beside the well. It was about the sixth hour. A woman from Samaria came to draw water. Jesus said to her, "Give me a drink." (For his disciples had gone away into the city to buy food.) The Samaritan woman said to him, "How is it that you, a Jew, ask for a drink from me, a woman of Samaria?" (For Jews have no dealings with Samaritans.) (John 4:1-9 ESV)*

Let's start with the last statement because it seems to be the thing that sparks the fire. It reads, *"For Jews have no dealings with Samaritans."* While this can certainly mean that they avoided contact with Samaritans, it does not have to mean that they also avoided traveling through their territory. Going from Jerusalem to Galilee through Samaria, instead of around it, could save several days or more of travel by foot. It is logical to think that someone who made the journey frequently would find ways to travel through Samaria and still avoid dealing with its inhabitants. This is not to say that logic trumps facts; it's to say that barring any real evidence of Jews avoiding travel through Samaria, logic must prevail. Let's continue to see if we find that evidence.

The next statement is, *"He had to pass through Samaria."* Many a sermon has been preached explaining that Jesus had to go through Samaria because He had a divine appointment with the Samaritan woman, and so this trip would have been an exception and not the norm. While this could be true, there is no evidence of it. It is easy to understand how someone would arrive at that conclusion since we assume (or know) that Jesus would have known that the woman would come there. Yet we must be careful when we apply this type of blanket logic when reading the Bible because it can lead us to see things that are simply not there. If we were to apply this type of thinking to Jesus' full ministry, we would be left wondering why Jesus did half the things He did. For example, before His arrest, we find Jesus praying to the Father and saying, *"If it be possible, let this cup pass from me."* Three times, He prayed that prayer. If we apply the "all-knowing" logic here, we would have to ask why Jesus did not know that there was no other possible way to save humanity.

We must stick to the text, then. And the text does not tell us that this meeting was a divine appointment. Samaria was not even Jesus' destination, Galilee was. The text tells us that the reason why Jesus was sitting by the well was because He was *wearied from His journey,* not because He was waiting for the woman to show up. This is not to argue that Jesus did not know He would meet this woman. The point is that the foreknowledge of the encounter did not necessarily fuel the decision to pass through Samaria. Considering the raw text, it is more likely that the author is simply letting the reader know that Jesus wound up in Sychar simply because His natural journey would take Him through Samaria.

Going into town

The next statement is the one in parenthesis about where the disciples were, *"(For his disciples had gone away into the city to buy food)."* This, too, is one of those statements that is preached beyond what the text says. Some claimed that the disciples were reluctant and displeased to have to go into town for food. Yet, that is nowhere in the text. It reads as quite ordinary and appropriate for them to tend to such a task. When they return, there is no grumbling, and nothing is mentioned concerning their dealings in town. Their only concern seems to be that Jesus is talking to a woman. The account ends by telling us that Jesus and His disciples stayed in Samaria for two more days. Not once do we read that anyone complained or objected.

Let us return to the first statement, *"For Jews have no dealings with Samaritans."* The unfortunate issue here is that we tend to read this literally when we should read it as a hyperbole, to be understood as an exaggeration the same way we say to someone, "You <u>never</u> listen to me." Our takeaway should not be that Jews never had dealings with Samaritans but that it was uncommon or avoided. The fact that the disciples went to town for food, the woman stayed to talk, the Samaritans welcomed Jesus and the disciples, and they stayed there for two days should tell us that reading that statement literally would be incorrect since all those acts required dealings with Samaritans.

Don't go to Samaria

We move our attention to another verse that is used to argue that Jews avoided traveling through Samaria. Matthew, Mark, and Luke record the account of when Jesus gave His disciples power and sent them out. In Matthew's account, we see this particular line:

> *These twelve Jesus sent out, instructing them, "Go nowhere among the Gentiles and enter no town of the Samaritans, (Matthew 10:5 ESV)*

It may be obvious, but we have to ask the question . . . if the Jews never traveled to or through Samaria, why would Jesus bother telling them not to go there? What would be the reason? It seems reasonable to surmise that Jesus instructed them not to go through Samaria for the same reason He instructed them not to go among the Gentiles, which was that Jesus came first for the Jews and that everyone else would be second. Telling His disciples to not enter Samaria had nothing to do with travel restrictions. Jesus was simply telling them to focus on the Jews.

More time in Samaria

Another account in the Book of Luke mentions Jesus being in the vicinity of Samaria, and it seems quite normal for Him to be there.

> *On the way to Jerusalem he was passing along between Samaria and Galilee. And as he entered a village, he was met by ten lepers, who stood at a distance and lifted up their voices, saying, "Jesus, Master, have mercy on us." When he saw them he said to them, "Go and show yourselves to the priests." And as they went they were cleansed. Then one of them, when he saw that he was healed,*

> *turned back, praising God with a loud voice; and he fell on his face at Jesus' feet, giving him thanks. Now he was a Samaritan. Then Jesus answered, "Were not ten cleansed? Where are the nine? Was no one found to return and give praise to God except this foreigner?" (Luke 17:11-18 ESV)*

Because we read about Jesus calling the Samaritan a foreigner, we assume that Jesus is in Jewish territory. That would mean that Jesus is in Galilee. But if that's true, why would Luke not just say that? Why say that Jesus is passing along Samaria and Galilee? Why mention Samaria at all?

Perhaps Luke is unsure of the exact location, and in his mind, it doesn't matter. Perhaps since Luke doesn't make a big deal about Jesus being near Samaria, neither should we. The picture that we can extrapolate from this account is that Jesus is in an area where Jews and Samaritans, near their borders, lived nearby and, therefore, could be commonly found together, as in the case of these ten lepers.

Some say that the text *"traveled between"* means that Jesus traveled through Galilee and then through Samaria. Some versions, such as the King James Version, use the word *midst* instead of *between* which makes it sound more convincing. As much as that would support the case that we are making in this chapter, it is less probable than saying that Jesus was traveling near their borders. If the author meant to tell us that Jesus traveled through these two regions, it would have been more appropriate to mention Galilee first and then Samaria since that is the order in which Jesus would have traveled on His way to Jerusalem. In any case, we see nothing in the text that even hints at traveling through Samaria as being a problem.

A Jewish historian

Flavius Josephus, the Jewish historian, mentions traveling through Samaria in several of his writings. Here are two excerpts from his works.

> *Now there arose a quarrel between the Samaritans and the Jews on the occasion following: It was the custom of the Galileans, when they came to the holy city at the festivals, to take their journeys through the country of the Samaritans; and at this time there lay, in the road they took, a village that was called Ginea, which was situated in the limits of Samaria and the great plain, where certain persons thereto belonging fought with the Galileans, and killed a great many of them. (The Antiquities of the Jews, 20.118)*

> *I then wrote to my friends in Samaria, to take care that they might safely pass through the country: for Samaria was already under the Romans, and it was absolutely necessary for those that go quickly [to Jerusalem] to pass through that country; for in that road you may, in three days' time go from Galilee to Jerusalem. (The Life of Flavius Josephus, 269)*

According to Josephus, travel through Samaria was not only necessary but customary.

Jewish writings

Rabbinic writings also confirm that Jewish Rabbis did travel to Samaria and had dealings with them. Whether the dealings were many or few is uncertain, but travel and dealings happened, nonetheless. Here are just two statements found in the Jerusalem Talmud Avodah Zarah 5:4.

> *Rebbi Ismael ben Rebbi Yose went to the well known Neapolis. The Samaritans came to him.*
>
> *Rebbi Jacob bar Aḥa in the name of Rebbi Hanina: It is permitted to lend to the Samaritans of Caesarea on interest.*

As points of reference, Neapolis was near Mt. Gerizim, which was the mountain that the Samaritans worshipped on, and Caesarea was a Samaritan town in the northwest corner near Galilee.

Other than the accounts mentioned here, the Bible mentions Samaria only two more times during the life of Jesus. Neither of those accounts mentions anything about Jewish travel.

In conclusion, while the teaching that Jews avoided travel through Samaria is prevalent, the evidence suggests otherwise. According to the Bible, our Jewish historian, Josephus, and Rabbinic writings, travel through Samaria seemed to have been quite normal.

SUMMARY

This chapter examines the common teaching that Jews in Jesus' time avoided traveling through Samaria.

- This teaching is based on the historical animosity between Jews and Samaritans due to intermarriage and the worship of other gods.

- The claim is that Jews would circumvent Samaria to avoid contact.

- The evidence presented in the Bible and historical sources is analyzed to determine the accuracy of this teaching.

- The Old Testament verses regarding Samaria refer not just to the city but to the entire northern kingdom, which includes many cities.

- The idea that Jews never traveled through Samaria is challenged with accounts from the New Testament, suggesting that they did, as well as references from Flavius Josephus and Rabbinic writings.

- The conclusion is that while the teaching of Jews avoiding Samaria is prevalent, the evidence suggests that travel through Samaria was not uncommon.

Conclusion

The standard teaching that Jews avoided traveling through Samaria due to hatred for Samaritans is not well-supported by the evidence. The Bible and historical sources indicate that travel through Samaria was not uncommon, suggesting that Jews did pass through this region.

Questions for Reflection or Group Study Discussion

1. Did the passages and arguments presented in this chapter change your view on the topic? Why or why not?

2. What passages had you not previously considered regarding this topic?

3. If your understanding was different than what was presented in this chapter, how was it different and how did you come to have that understanding?

4. Regardless of your final position on the topic (agree or disagree), did you learn anything new? If so, what?

Methodology

This section outlines the methods that I use while studying to extract the most reasonable interpretation of scripture as presented in the Bible.

Questions

The worst thing we can do when reading the Bible is not to ask questions. This sounds obvious, but for those who have been churchgoers for a long time, I find this is one of their biggest problems in achieving correct interpretation. The questions are often not asked because they have just enough information to reach easy conclusions, whether they are correct or not.

Of the many questions I ask of a passage or topic, the most impactful is, "Does it say what I think it says, and can I prove it with scripture?" Followed by, "Is there an opposing view, and can I reconcile them?"

Consistency

I've employed a strict methodology to ensure that the same discovery rules are applied to all topics. To help explain what they are, I will use an actual case and refer to it throughout.

Proving (or disproving) the most common understanding

Let's take the word *paradise* as our example. The most common belief is that it refers to heaven. And so we ask the question, does the Bible support that?

Finding every mention

The first step in the process is to find every instance of the word *paradise* in the Bible. This is followed by examining each instance for its specific meaning within the context of the chapter. This part can be tricky because I must pay special attention to what is actually being said and put aside what I have been conditioned to think it says.

Avoiding Presuppositions

For example, the first occurrence of the word *paradise* is found in the Book of Luke, where Jesus tells the thief on the cross next to Him, *"Truly I tell you, today you will be with me in paradise."* We assume Jesus means heaven because we have been conditioned to think that paradise means heaven. But what it really says is paradise, not heaven. In fact, the word heaven does not appear at all in this chapter.

We then might conclude that since Jesus ascended to heaven, He must have referred to heaven when He said paradise. However, Jesus did not ascend to heaven on the day He died; He ascended three days later. If we conclude that Jesus was telling the thief that on that specific day, he would be joining Him in heaven, then we would have to admit that Jesus lied to the thief since it took Jesus three days to get there. And since Jesus lying to the thief is less likely to have occurred, then we must table the idea that paradise is heaven until we find better evidence. In this example, what I've done is strip away what it does not say to expose only what it does say, even if its true meaning is still unclear.

Examine and re-examine

This is a continuous process. With each perceived conclusion, the same question is asked again, "Does it really say that?" Once I strip out all assumptions and establish what the text says (and does not say) to the best of my ability, I compare all occurrences to see where they differ or are similar. This exposes themes in thought and even terminology usage.

In the case of *paradise*, the task is not so daunting since the word *paradise* only appears in the Bible three times and only in the New Testament.

Fighting the urge

By this time, I have enough evidence to start formulating some conclusions, and it is at this point that I apply the brakes. I have a mantra that I recite to myself; it is short and simple, "Fight the urge." The urge is to jump to those conclusions hastily without considering what the many who have come before me have to say, those who have spent their lives doing exactly what I'm doing, searching for the truth.

Outside input and considerations

I know that nothing will derail me faster than thinking that my brain is better than all others, so my next step is to study what others have found and have concluded and compare that to what I've found. Mostly, I want to know how they arrived at their conclusions and what perspective they have that I might have missed.

Tackle opposing views

When I find an opposing view, I examine their assumptions based on the Bible verses they chose to support their conclusions while equally considering the verses they have ignored. My goal here is to prove one view with great certainty — considering all verses on the topic and not just those that support one view. As we witnessed above, had we ignored the verses that tell us that Jesus did not ascend to heaven right away, we would have been led to incorrect conclusions about where the thief went when he died.

Weighing verses

We often find ourselves looking at two or more verses seemingly contradicting each other. In this case, it is important to weigh each verse out. In the case of the word *paradise*, Jesus tells Mary three days after His death that He had not yet ascended to the Father. So, which is correct, did Jesus go to heaven with the thief the day He died, or had He been somewhere else for three days? The verse that Jesus says that He had not yet been to heaven (to the Father) carries more weight because it is a direct testimony and is less ambiguous than the verse that mentions paradise. When there is an absolute lack of reconciliation between verses, the weightier is assumed to prevail. I say assumed because weight is just one factor to be considered, albeit one of the most critical factors.

Accounting for change over time

Although this does not apply to the word *paradise*, it is worth mentioning as part of the methodology process.

Several Biblical ideas were gradually solidified over time. We tend to forget that the Bible was not written in one day or year. It accounts for a history spanning thousands of years of societies growing in knowledge and understanding, forming new ideas, and progressing in almost all areas of their existence.

Let's take the case of when a blind Paul was visited by Ananias, whom Jesus had sent. After Ananias gives Paul the intended message, notice what else he says to Paul.

> *And now why do you wait? Rise and be baptized and wash away your sins, calling on his name. (Acts 22:16 ESV)*

Here, we see that in Ananias' mind, baptism, while no longer John's baptism, was still considered as having the purpose of washing away sins. But by the time we get to the account in Acts 19, where Paul ran into the disciples in Ephesus some 20 years later, we can see that Paul understood that baptism was no longer for the forgiveness of sins.

This is not just concerning baptism but many other things. Even the disciples' understanding changed over time. What they thought about Jesus and His ministry in year one with Him differed from what they understood in year three. After receiving the Holy Spirit, after Jesus' ascension, they understood even more. But even then, their understanding was not complete. We can see this in the account of Peter being called to Cornelius' house and learning about the inclusion of Gentiles into God's plan.

The point is that when studying scripture, we must consider the progression of change in culture and understanding that naturally happens over time and how new ideas grow and are solidified, for how sad it would be if we allowed our first-grade understanding to trump our more mature adult minds. In the case of our comparison of Ananias and Paul, having two verses that define the purpose of baptism differently, we can conclude that Paul has the correct meaning of baptism.

About the Author

E.O. Valle, born in 1961 in Brooklyn, New York, embarked on a unique life journey that shaped his dedication to studying and teaching biblical principles. After residing in Puerto Rico for five years, the place of his parents' origin, he eventually settled in New Jersey, where he spent most of his life before relocating to Florida in 2021.

He holds an undergraduate degree in Divinity, which supports his unwavering commitment to exploring the intricacies of scripture, the knowledge of God, and its profound influence on individuals. He has spent the better part of the last decade crafting Bible studies and facilitating small-group learning experiences.

He is the creator of Bible Dose, an online platform designed for group Bible study to help churches manage their study groups, content, and discipleship strategies.

He is the founder of My Neighbor PR, a non-profit organization that was started in response to the devastation caused in Puerto Rico by Hurricane Maria in 2017, where he served as Executive Director for several years.

His spiritual foundation reflects a multifaceted upbringing. While his mother was a devout Christian, his father did not share the same faith. It was his mother who instilled in him the importance of faith and ensured its prominent place in his life. Like many young adults, he strayed from his Christian upbringing for many years, only to rediscover its significance later in life. Today, his mission is to provide direction, education, and guidance to all who seek a deeper connection with the Word of God.

His love language is quality time. Don't buy him a gift, don't send him a card. Instead, invite him out to dinner; he might even pick up the check.

**Thank you for reading
That's Not What The Bible Says.**

For access to the free companion Bible Study Library,
please visit www.eovalle.com

FREE COMPANION
Bible Study Library!

Congratulations on completing "That's Not What the Bible Says," your guide to reading the Bible with clarity and insight. But your journey doesn't end here – it's just beginning!

You now have access to the Companion Bible Study Library, absolutely FREE! Dive deeper into the Word and enrich your understanding with dozens of short, thought-provoking Bible studies.

For Small Group Leaders:
Are you a small group leader seeking fresh, engaging Bible study ideas? Look no further! This library is a treasure trove of resources to inspire meaningful discussions and spiritual growth within your group.

For the Seekers of Truth:
Whether you're a seasoned Bible scholar or simply curious about the scriptures, this library is your gateway to a deeper relationship with God's Word.

Don't miss out on this incredible resource. It's my gift to you, because I believe that the Word of God should be accessible to all who seek it.

Together, let's explore the depths of God's Word and grow in faith and understanding.

Visit **www.eovalle.com** to get started today!

Made in the USA
Las Vegas, NV
18 January 2024

84541626R00125